MUIR
AMONG THE
ANIMALS

Portrait of Muir: John Muir Papers, Holt-Atherton Center
for Western Studies, University of the Pacific.

MUIR
AMONG THE
ANIMALS

*The Wildlife Writings
of John Muir*

LISA MIGHETTO

EDITOR

SIERRA CLUB BOOKS

The Sierra Club, founded in 1892 by John Muir, has devoted itself to the study and protection of the earth's scenic and ecological resources—mountains, wetlands, woodlands, wild shores and rivers, deserts and plains. The publishing program of the Sierra Club offers books to the public as a nonprofit educational service in the hope that they may enlarge the public's understanding of the Club's basic concerns. The point of view expressed in each book, however, does not necessarily represent that of the Club. The Sierra Club has some sixty chapters coast to coast, in Canada, Hawaii, and Alaska. For information about how you may participate in its programs to preserve wilderness and the quality of life, please address inquiries to Sierra Club, 730 Polk Street, San Francisco, CA 94109.

Animal Death, The Passenger Pigeon and *The Shrike* are excerpted from THE STORY OF MY BOYHOOD AND YOUTH by John Muir. Copyright 1912 and 1913 by the Atlantic Monthly Company. Copyright 1913 by John Muir. Copyright 1916 by Houghton Mifflin Company. Copyright renewed 1940 and 1941 by Wanda Muir Hanna. Reprinted by permission of Houghton Mifflin Company. *Anthropocentrism and Predation* is excerpted from A THOUSAND MILE WALK TO THE GULF by John Muir. Copyright 1916 by Houghton Mifflin Company. Copyright renewed 1944 by Ellen Muir Funk. Reprinted by permission of Houghton Mifflin Company.

LIBRARY OF CONGRESS CATALOGING-IN-PUBLICATION DATA

Muir, John, 1838–1914.
Muir among the animals.

Bibliography: p. 195
1. Zoology—Collected works. I. Mighetto, Lisa,
1955–   .   II. Title.
QL3.M85   1986   590   86–3914
ISBN 0–87156–607–9

Cover and book design by Wilsted & Taylor
Printed in the United States of America
10 9 8 7 6 5 4 3 2 1

TO MY PARENTS,
for their love of animals,
and TO MY MOTHER- AND FATHER-IN-LAW,
for their interest in John Muir

Contents

Acknowledgments

For their aid, I thank Blaine P. Lamb, Kirsten E. Lewis, and Ronald H. Limbaugh of the Holt-Atherton Center for Western Studies at the University of the Pacific. I am indebted also to the staffs of the Bancroft Library in Berkeley, the Haggin Museum in Stockton, the John Muir National Historic Site in Martinez, and the Yosemite Research Library. Although they were not involved directly with this project, George K. Behlmer, Alfred Runte, and Lewis O. Saum provided me with valuable advice about research and writing; Michael P. Cohen and Thomas R. Dunlap generously offered their ideas on American perceptions of wildlife. Financial support was granted by the Rachel Royston Permanent Scholarship Foundation. Above all, I am grateful for the assistance of Frank L. Mighetto.

Thus godlike sympathy grows and thrives
and spreads far beyond the teachings of
churches and schools, where too often
the mean, blinding, loveless doctrine is
taught that animals have neither mind nor
soul, have no rights that we are bound
to respect, and were made only for man,
to be petted, spoiled, slaughtered,
or enslaved.

JOHN MUIR
The Story of My Boyhood and Youth

Editor's Preface

John Muir and the Rights of Animals

No late nineteenth-century writer was a more eloquent observer of wildlife than John Muir. "Any glimpse into the life of an animal," he explained, "quickens our own and makes it so much the larger and better in every way."[1] Muir, whose name has long been associated with mountain scenery, recognized that wild creatures are an essential component of wilderness. His writings not only familiarized readers with the habits of animals, but also encouraged them to consider the natural world from a new perspective. (Although some of the scientific nomenclature has changed since Muir's day, his text, for the most part, has not been altered.)

Muir's appreciation for what he called his "horizontal

Portions of this essay first appeared in *Sierra*, March/April 1985, and *Pacific Historian* 29 (Summer/Fall 1985).

brothers" went far beyond that of his contemporaries. Although concern for wildlife increased in his day, much of the impetus came from practical-minded sportsmen who wanted to protect game. Several historians have pointed out that this group comprised a large portion of the early conservation movement.[2] Rarely, however, did Muir have a good word for hunters. Summing up their utilitarian rationale for preservation, he wryly noted that "the pleasure of killing is in danger of being lost from there being little or nothing left to kill." Muir, on the other hand, hoped for a "recognition of the rights of animals and their kinship to ourselves."[3]

While it is true Muir himself shot wild creatures as a youth in Wisconsin and later accompanied hunting expeditions in the Sierra, he had no liking for the "murder business" and rarely carried firearms. Blood sports, he argued, were a debasing pastime, capable of transforming even "the decent gentleman or devout saint" into "a howling, bloodthirsty, demented savage." Neither did he approve of angling, which encouraged people to seek "pleasure in the pain of fishes struggling for their lives." Such activity, in Muir's estimation, was inappropriate in the "Yosemite temple," for it violated the "rights of animals." At times this aversion to blood sports took the form of subtle ridicule. Lacking regard for the character and intelligence of their prey, hunters, he claimed, remained unaware that they were "themselves hunted by animals," who "in perfect safety follow them out of curiosity."[4]

Slaughtering for food also bothered him. Repulsed by

✳ John Muir and the Rights of Animals ✳

the "depraved appetite" that craved meat, Muir, like Thoreau, preferred "bread without flesh"—at least while in the Sierra. Man, he lamented at several points in his journal, "seems to be the only animal whose food soils him"; ideally, "one ought to be trained and tempered to enjoy life . . . in full independence of any particular kind of nourishment."[5] Such squeamishness, coming from a person who reveled in wildness, stemmed from more than a simple offense to a delicate sensibility: Muir's distaste was in keeping with his denial of the natural world's brutality. Unlike many conservationists, he was concerned with the protection of *individual* animals as well as species.

Of course, Muir's sensitivity to the suffering of wild animals was not unique. During his lifetime, a "comparatively modern social manifestation"—labeled by one Victorian commentator as the "new humanitarianism"—flourished on both sides of the Atlantic, giving rise to numerous animal welfare organizations. What distinguished the late nineteenth century from previous eras was an increasing awareness of pain.[6]

Accordingly, capacity for feeling became a basis for the protection of animals, both wild and domestic. "Erase sentiency from the universe," suggested animal rights advocate J. Howard Moore, "and you erase the possibility of ethics."[7] Unlike many turn-of-the-century preservationists, humanitarians objected to the killing of wild creatures not because it was wasteful, but because it inflicted suffering. Although concerned primarily with animals in urban areas, the Society for the Prevention of Cruelty to Animals

* John Muir and the Rights of Animals *

(SPCA) protested the wholesale slaughter of western wild-life and urged Congress to create a department for the protection of such animals as the buffalo. Henry Bergh, who established the group in this country, exemplified the link between humanitarians and preservationists by becoming the first vice president of the Audubon Society.[8]

Similarly, Henry Salt, a leading English humanitarian whose works were read and debated in the United States, denounced cruelty to wild creatures. Entire chapters of his book *Animals' Rights* (1892) were devoted to "amateur butchery" and "murderous millenry"—Salt's terms for sport and fashion. He portrayed the liberation of animals as an inevitable extension of the same spirit that granted rights to slaves and women. To him, vegetarianism was an essential step in this progression: it is not possible, he argued, to assert the rights of an animal "on whom you propose to make a meal."[9] Muir, too, wondered at the inconsistency of "preaching, praying men and women" who killed and ate animals "while eloquently discoursing on the coming of the blessed, peaceful, bloodless millennium."[10]

These views, which formed Salt's "creed of kinship," owed much to nineteenth-century science. The link between man and other animals being affirmed, Salt contended that nearly all creatures possess a sense of morality and an aesthetic sensibility, along with a character of their own. They should enjoy a "restricted freedom," he concluded, allowing them "individual development." So bent was Salt on according liberty to animals that he opposed keeping them as pets or in zoos—a practice that implied subservience and smacked of condescension. Few people would delight in a captive animal, he claimed, "if they . . . fully considered how blighted and sterilized a life it must be." Moreover, to prevent the tendency to regard animals as "things," Salt suggested that we refrain from the pronoun *it* when referring to them. The term *vermin*, when applied to "rabbits, rats, and other small animals," further offended him, for "the application of a contemptuous name" encouraged cruelty."[11]

Such ideas were not widely accepted in turn-of-the-century America, where the "new humanitarianism" affected only a small portion of the population. Salt himself was derided as being a "compendium of the cranks."[12] Muir did not align himself with humanitarians or comment on Salt's works. Yet the attitudes of the two men toward the animal world were similar: throughout his writings, Muir emphasized the intelligence and individuality of wildlife.

This respect took years to develop. Upon first arriving in the Sierra, Muir in fact "lacked the right manners of the wilderness." His initial encounter with a bear, however, provided him some animal etiquette. Sighting one of these animals in the Sierra was a rare opportunity, for they were especially elusive in the days before large numbers of visitors flocked to campgrounds, generating attractive garbage. Hence, he was eager to make the most of his "interview" with the "big cinnamon." After studying the bear from a distance, Muir, wanting to observe the animal's gait, rushed forward, shouting and waving his arms.

❋ John Muir and the Rights of Animals ❋

The bear, however, not only refused to run but also indicated a willingness to fight. His mistake thus made "monstrously plain," Muir "began to fear that on myself would fall the work of running." To his relief, the bear eventually withdrew into the forest. "I was glad to part with him," Muir confessed. His subsequent meetings with bears were marked by caution and humility: when he encountered a "formidable" grizzly, Muir hid behind a tree, hoping to escape notice. In any case, his fright did not keep him from observing the "fine dignity" of the animal.[13]

Muir later advised tourists in the Sierra to adopt a similar approach to wildlife. Answering frequent complaints about the scarcity of animals in the Yosemite Valley, he pointed out that large groups of boisterous people tend to alarm wild creatures. "Even the frightened pines would run away if they could," he explained. But if travelers "would go singly, without haste or noise, away from the region of trails and pack trains, they would speedily learn that these mountain mansions are not without inhabitants, many of whom, confiding and gentle, would be glad to make their acquaintance." In fact, Muir's animals often sought *him* out, displaying the "liveliest curiosity."[14]

Like Salt, Muir believed these wild creatures possessed unique characters. Our conceit, he argued, prevents us from perceiving their individuality. While his fellow nature writer John Burroughs maintained that animals are guided solely by instinct, Muir emphasized their refinement and nobility in his own writings. *The Story of My Boyhood and Youth* (1913), for instance, recalled the "wonderful sympathy" and "self-sacrificing devotion" of a wild goose who attacked Muir in defense of another bird he had shot. In this passage, which recounted one of Muir's "strangest hunting experiences," it was the goose who emerged as the admirable character.[15]

In his early years, though, Muir's esteem did not include animals brought into the mountains by man. Exasperating experiences from his shepherding days had convinced him of the stupidity of these creatures: "A [domestic] sheep," he concluded, "can hardly be called an animal," for "an entire flock is required to make one foolish individual." Moreover, Muir found tame sheep to be far less graceful than their wild cousins, whom he considered to be "the best mountaineers of all." This theme was developed in his essay "Wild Wool" (1875), in which he demonstrated the superiority of mountain animals to those of the lowlands.[16]

Not only did domestic sheep lack character as far as Muir was concerned, but these "hoofed locusts" also destroyed the vegetation of mountain meadows. In contrast, "nature's cattle and poultry"—deer, sheep, and flocks of grouse—left their "mountain gardens" unmarred. Writing in the 1870s, before predator elimination had created overpopulation of deer, Muir claimed that these "dainty feeders" did not crush the flowers and grass in the Sierra. Instead, they pruned the vegetation, "keeping it in order." All wild animals, from agile sheep to broad-footed bears, "beautify the ground on which they walk, picturing it with their awe-inspiring tracks."[17]

❋ John Muir and the Rights of Animals ❋

Later in his life, Muir revised his assessment of tame creatures. At his ranch in Martinez, he kept a variety of pets, including cats, dogs, and a screech owl. "I suppose that almost any wild animal may be made a pet," he wrote. His most celebrated animal essay featured the dog Stickeen, who accompanied him on a harrowing excursion across an Alaskan glacier. As night was falling, the two encountered an enormous crevasse, passable only by means of a precarious ice-sliver bridge. At first reluctant to follow Muir across, the terrified dog finally reached the opposite side of the chasm. Safe at last, he "ran and cried and barked and rolled about fairly hysterical in the sudden revulsion from the depths of despair to triumphant joy." This shared ordeal, which was to become Muir's "most memorable" experience in the wilderness, poignantly illustrates the appeal of his animal portrayals. Stickeen "enlarged my life," Muir wrote, for "through him as through a window I have ever since been looking with deeper sympathy into all my fellow mortals."[18] His change in perspective was reflected throughout *The Story of My Boyhood and Youth*, one of his last literary efforts.

Written for boys, this work was designed to instill a respect for all creatures. Although the young Muir had delighted in tormenting cats, the book pointed out, he had also developed an early appreciation for birds. Projecting his reverence for living things back to his childhood, Muir also offered sympathetic portraits of farm animals from his Wisconsin days. These portrayals, which emphasized the near-human qualities of animals, repudiated the "loveless doctrine" that they have "neither mind nor soul."[19]

Each animal in the book thus had an "individual character." Buck, for one, was a "notably sagacious fellow" who "seemed to reason sometimes almost like ourselves." Although at feeding time the other cattle had to have their pumpkins split open for them, this resourceful ox crushed them himself with his head. "He went to the pile," Muir explained, "picked out a good one, like a boy choosing an orange or apple, rolled it down on to the open ground, deliberately kneeled in front of it, placed his broad, flat brow on top of it, brought his weight hard down and crushed it, then quietly arose and went on with his meal in comfort." This action, Muir was careful to indicate, derived not from "blind instinct," but from intelligence. When hungry, another ox who lived by his wits was given to "opening all the fences that stood in his way to the cornfields."[20]

The Story of My Boyhood and Youth also had its share of dog stories. One of these was a variation of the tale of the "noble, faithful" canine who, after defending a child against a wild beast, was mistaken for the attacker and unjustly slain. Similarly, Watch, the family dog, was an admirable creature who "could not read books" but "could read faces," and "was a good judge of character." In fact, Muir's affection for dogs preceded his acceptance of other domestic animals: in his journal in the 1870s, he praised his canine companion Carlo for his "wonderful intelligence."[21]

* John Muir and the Rights of Animals *

The message here was clear: Muir wanted to convince his young readers that animals should be treated respectfully. His book not only extolled the virtues of farm animals, but also deplored their abuse by humans. Muir looked forward to "a better time" when people would become "truly humane, and learn to put their animal fellow mortals in their hearts instead of on their backs or in their dinners." His aim, then, was comparable to that of the humanitarians, for he, too, believed that animals should be regarded as "fellow citizens."[22]

When it came to predators, though, Muir parted company with the humanitarian movement. While its adherents were kind to "desirable" animals, they were intolerant of seemingly bloodthirsty creatures who were cruel to their fellows or posed a threat to man. Carnivores who did not live by humanitarian principles were deemed unworthy of protection. Henry Bergh, for instance, threatened P. T. Barnum with prosecution for feeding live rabbits to snakes. When the circus caretakers pointed out to the SPCA leader that these animals eat only live prey, Bergh suggested that the "hateful reptiles" be allowed to starve. So serious was this humanitarian that Barnum's people were forced to convey the snakes in suitcases across the border to New Jersey—away from SPCA jurisdiction—for feeding.[23] Even Salt, the most radical and vocal of the animal rights advocates, did not extend his goodwill to "wolves, and other dangerous species."[24] Another vegetarian who found bestiality repugnant hoped to "let the wolf and tiger die."[25] Objections to meat-eating pets were also raised among humanitarians, who continued to publish leaflets outlining vegetarian diets for dogs and cats.[26]

Conservationists shared the humanitarians' dim view of predators. William T. Hornaday, director of the New York Zoological Park, suggested in 1913 that "several species of birds," all hawks, be "at once put under sentence of death for their destructiveness of useful birds." Owls, although under "grave suspicion," were saved from "instant condemnation" by "the delightful amount of rats, mice, moles, gophers and noxious insects they annually consume." The pilot blacksnake—"long, thick and truculent"—seemed to Hornaday to be particularly "deserving of death." Another "bad" animal, to his mind, was the domestic cat, who preyed on squirrels and birds in his zoo. Some grizzlies, too, belonged to "the pest class." But wolves were the "most despicable" of predators. "There is no depth of meanness, treachery or cruelty," Hornaday explained, "to which they do not cheerfully descend."[27] Such statements, indicating Hornaday's utilitarian bent as well as his hatred of predators, were not unusual: Theodore Roosevelt, the great conservationist president, similarly denounced the wolf as being "the archetype of ravin, the beast of waste and desolation."[28] The coyote, on the other hand, was sometimes characterized as a cowardly varmint, "a pariah whose name is an insult when applied to a man, be he ever so low."[29] This disdain was translated into policy; even the National Park Service and the Audubon Society advocated the elimination of predators on their lands.[30] The war against wolves in present-day Alaska demonstrates that old attitudes die hard.

In contrast to humanitarians and conservationists, Muir presented all wild creatures favorably. Rattlesnakes, traditionally regarded as dangerous and repulsive, were, in his estimation, "downright bashful" and deserving of respect. Lizards, too, were "gentle and guileless" creatures with "beautiful eyes, expressing the clearest innocence, so that, in spite of the prejudices brought from cool, lizardless countries, one must soon learn to like them." Moreover, Muir delighted in the company of a variety of insects, including flies.[31]

Neither did he condemn larger meat-eaters for their apparently cruel habits. In *Our National Parks* (1901), Muir marveled at the number of animals a bear can consume. "In this happy land no famine comes nigh him," he observed. "What digestion! A sheep or wounded deer or a pig he eats warm, about as quickly as a boy eats a buttered muffin; or should the meat be a month old, it still is welcomed with tremendous relish." Though Muir viewed this scene with a degree of squeamishness, there is no judgment reflected in his words. He in fact regretted that these "good-natured" animals were hunted.[32]

This inclination appears stronger in a mischievous and disconcerting passage from his *A Thousand-Mile Walk to the Gulf* (1916), which notes that alligators should be "blessed now and then with a mouthful of terror-stricken man by way of dainty." In his original journal, these sentiments were reinforced by Muir's drawing (which did not appear in the published version) of an alligator eating a man while another saurian looked on with approval. Also unpublished were his praises of the coyote, a "beautiful" and "graceful" animal persecuted for its supposed taste for mutton.[33] Because many turn-of-the-century readers would not have approved of Muir's position, his wildlife portrayals that appeared in print featured such "inoffensive" animals as deer, squirrels, and nonpredatory birds.

Muir's acceptance of carnivores was in part linked to his denial of their brutality. Lamenting the "dismal irreverence" with which humans viewed the animal world, he found their talk of "ferocious beasts" to be morbid. To him, all nature was beneficent; the woods were full of "happy birds and beasts," none of whom was "[f]ierce and cruel." Alligators and snakes were not "mysterious evils," he argued. Neither were Muir's animals subject to the bloody teeth and claws envisioned by Darwinists: "I never saw one drop of blood," he reported, "on all this wilderness."[34]

There is little animal suffering, then, described in Muir's writings. His wild creatures experienced "[n]ot a headache or any other ache amongst them." Young birds, he imagined, enjoyed an ideal home life, for they were "protected [by both father and mother] and fed and to some extent educated." Muir's ouzel—the subject of "The Humming-Bird of the California Water-Falls" (1878), one of his best-known animal essays—died without "gloom," vanishing "like a flower, or a foam-bell at the foot of a waterfall." Another of his favorites, the Douglas squirrel, was depicted as being "as free from disease as a sunbeam." Even his grasshopper was a "jolly fellow," full of "glad, hilarious energy." In the life of this insect, "every day is a holiday; and when at length his sun sets, . . . he will cuddle down on the forest floor and die like the leaves and the flowers, leaving no unsightly remains for burial."[35]

It would be a mistake, however, to label Muir's view of the animal world sentimental. For all his observations of benevolence, he recognized that wild creatures can be dangerous: throughout his travels, Muir recorded his fear of bears, wolves, and alligators. But unlike his contemporaries, he refused to evaluate animal behavior by man's standards. "[I]t is right," Muir claimed, that creatures "make use of one another"; what bothered him was the spirit in which most humans use other animals. The egocentric assurance that the earth was made only for the pleasure and convenience of humans is "not supported by the facts," he argued in his journal. (In the published version, this passage was amended to read "by all the facts.") What about the carnivores, he asked, who "smack their lips over raw man?" Speculation on the purpose of these troublesome beasts irritated Muir, who could not see why man should "value himself as more than a small part of the one great unit of creation."[36]

Such sentiments have earned Muir an association with modern-day biocentrism. Perceiving the interconnectedness of living things, he noted the importance of maintaining ecological balance. Like Aldo Leopold, who recognized the need for an "ecological conscience," Muir denounced predator control: in one unpublished essay describing a jackrabbit hunt in the San Joaquin Valley, he pointed out that ranchers would not be plagued by the overpopulation of rodents had they not destroyed the "snakes and hawks and coyotes." Yet Muir differed from biocentrists in his emphasis upon the singularity of animals. Leopold, for example, was more concerned in the 1930s and 1940s with the health of the biotic community than with the welfare of individual creatures. In contrast, Muir was convinced that despite "universal union there is a division sufficient in degree for the purposes of the most intense individuality; no matter, therefore, what may be the note which any creature forms in the song of existence, it is made first for itself, then more and more remotely for all the world and worlds." Each animal, he concluded, has "rights that we are bound to respect."[37]

Muir's "intense love of animals" was, according to his friend, paleontologist Henry Fairfield Osborn, one of his striking characteristics.[38] So strong was his interest that in 1910 he began writing another animal book, which was never completed; several of the unpublished essays appear in this volume. Certainly the uniqueness of Muir's subjects, which he believed to be essential to their "pure wildness," added to the charm of his writings.[39] "His accounts of the bird or animal which got next to his heart," wrote one turn-of-the-century observer, "can never fail to find

readers and hold them with . . . tenderest interest."[40]
As Americans adopt an increasingly respectful attitude
toward animals, Muir's portrayals will continue to grow in
appeal.

NOTES

1. Linnie Marsh Wolfe, ed., *John of the Mountains* (Boston: Houghton
Mifflin, 1915), p. 277. So far, studies of Muir have devoted little space to his
portrayal of animals. Stephen Fox's *John Muir and His Legacy: The American
Conservation Movement* (Boston: Little, Brown, 1981), Michael P. Cohen's
The Pathless Way: John Muir and American Wilderness (Madison: University of
Wisconsin Press, 1984), and Frederick Turner's *Rediscovering America: John
Muir in His Time and Ours* (New York: Viking, 1985) do not consider the
subject in much depth.

2. John F. Reiger, *American Sportsmen and the Origin of Conservation* (New
York: Winchester Press, 1975), and James B. Trefethen, *An American Crusade
for Wildlife* (New York: Winchester Press, 1975).

3. Edwin Way Teale, ed., *The Wilderness World of John Muir* (Boston:
Houghton Mifflin, 1954), p. 314.

4. As early as 1872, Muir wrote about the rights of animals in an unpublished essay entitled "Bears." (John Muir Papers, Holt-Atherton Center for
Western Studies, University of the Pacific, Stockton, Calif.) See also William
Frederic Bade, ed., *Steep Trails* (Boston: Houghton Mifflin, 1918), pp. 45,
50; John Muir, *My First Summer in the Sierra* (Boston: Houghton Mifflin,
1916), p. 190; Teale, *Wilderness World*, p. 314.

5. Wolfe, *John of the Mountains*, p. 97; Muir, *My First Summer*, pp. 78–79.

6. Thomas Stanley, "The New Humanitarianism," *Westminster Review*
155 (April 1901): 414–23. See also John Henry Barrows, "The Spirit of
Humanity," *Independent* 51, December 28, 1899, p. 3468, and James Turner,
Reckoning with the Beast: Animals, Pain, and Humanity in the Victorian Mind
(Baltimore: Johns Hopkins University Press, 1980).

7. J. Howard Moore, *Better-World Philosophy: A Sociological Synthesis*
(Chicago: Charles H. Kerr, 1899; 1906). See also idem, *The Universal Kinship* (Chicago: Charles H. Kerr, 1908).

8. Zulma Steele, *Angel in Top Hat* (New York: Harper and Brothers, 1942), p. 278.

9. Henry Salt, *Animals' Rights* (New York: Macmillan, 1892), pp. 43, 94. See also George Hendrick, *Henry Salt: Humanitarian Reformer and Man of Letters* (Urbana: University of Illinois Press, 1977).

10. John Muir, *The Story of My Boyhood and Youth* (1913; reprint ed., Madison: University of Wisconsin Press, 1965), p. 69.

11. Salt, *Animals' Rights*, pp. 22, 42, 60.

12. Stephen Winsten, *Salt and His Circle* (New York: Hutchinson, 1951), p. 67.

13. John Muir, *Our National Parks* (Boston: Houghton Mifflin, 1901), pp. 174–78.

14. Ibid., pp. 213, 222; Frederic R. Gunsky, ed., *South of Yosemite: Selected Writings of John Muir* (Garden City, N.Y.: Natural History Press, 1968), p. 182.

15. Muir, *My Boyhood and Youth*, p. 122.

16. Muir, *My First Summer*, p. 114; Gunsky, *South of Yosemite*, p. 131; Bade, *Steep Trails*, pp. 3–18.

17. Gunsky, *South of Yosemite*, p. 173.

18. Muir's pets were described in Sally Johnson Ketcham's interview with Helen Funk Muir, recounted in the Furnishing Plan (1971) for the John Muir National Historic Site, Martinez, Calif. See also Muir, *My Boyhood and Youth*, p. 149; Wolfe, *John of the Mountains*, p. 277; and John Muir, *Travels in Alaska* (Boston: Houghton Mifflin, 1915), p. 256.

19. Muir, *My Boyhood and Youth*, p. 89.

20. Ibid., pp. 74–75.

21. The story of Llewellyn's dog is recounted in far more detail in the Pelican Bay manuscript—the original version of this work—at the University of the Pacific, Stockton, Calif. See also Muir, *My Boyhood and Youth*, pp. 6, 66; idem, *My First Summer*, p. 6.

22. Muir, *My Boyhood and Youth*, p. 145; Muir, *Travels in Alaska*, p. 256.

23. Steele, *Angel in Top Hat*, pp. 236–37.

24. Salt, *Animals' Rights*, p. 54.

25. Howard Williams, *The Ethics of Diet: A Biographical History of the Literature of Humane Dietetics, from the Earliest Period to the Present Day* (London: Swan Sonnenschein, 1896), title page.

26. Peter Singer, *Animal Liberation: A New Ethics for Our Treatment of Animals* (New York: New York Review Book, 1975), p. 252. See also Steele, *Angel in Top Hat*, pp. 189–90.

27. William T. Hornaday, *Our Vanishing Wildlife: Its Extermination and*

* John Muir and the Rights of Animals *

Preservation (New York: New York Zoological Society, 1913), pp. 80–81; idem, *Wild Animal Round-Up: Stories and Pictures from the Passing Show* (New York: Charles Scribner's Sons, 1925), p. 281; idem, *The American Natural History* (New York: Charles Scribner's Sons, 1904), p. 22. See also idem, *The Minds and Manners of Wild Animals: A Book of Personal Observations* (New York: Charles Scribner's Sons, 1922), p. 223.

28. As quoted in Stanley Paul Young, *The Wolf in North American History* (Caldwell, Idaho: Caxton Printers, 1946), p. 29.

29. Edwin L. Sabin, "The Coyote," *Overland Monthly* 51 (May 1908): 474.

30. Joseph Grinnell, "Animal Life as an Asset to National Parks," *Science*, 15 September 1916, p. 378. See also Donald Worster, *Nature's Economy: The Roots of Ecology* (San Francisco: Sierra Club Books, 1977), pp. 258–90 ("The Value of a Varmint"), and Thomas R. Dunlap, "Values for Varmints: Predator Control and Environmental Ideas, 1920–1939," *Pacific Historical Review* 53 (May 1984): 145.

31. Muir, *Our National Parks*, pp. 204, 208; idem, *My First Summer*, p. 142.

32. Muir, *Our National Parks*, pp. 172–73; Gunsky, *South of Yosemite*, p. 119.

33. John Muir, Florida and Cuba journal; idem, coyote manuscript, John Muir Papers, University of the Pacific, Stockton, Calif. One brief paragraph concerning the coyote appeared in John Muir's "Twenty Hill Hollow," *Overland Monthly* 9 (July 1872): 83.

34. Muir, *A Thousand-Mile Walk to the Gulf* (Boston: Houghton Mifflin, 1916), p. 98; Wolfe, *John of the Mountains*, pp. 82, 93. See also Lisa Mighetto, "Science, Sentiment, and Anxiety: American Nature Writing at the Turn of the Century," *Pacific Historical Review* 54 (February 1985): 33–50, and Cohen, *The Pathless Way*, pp. 179–81.

35. Muir, *My First Summer*, pp. 68, 96, 139–41; Wolfe, *John of the Mountains*, p. 165.

36. Muir, *Thousand-Mile Walk*, pp. 136–39.

37. Muir, "Animals," John Muir Papers, University of the Pacific, Stockton, Calif.; idem, *My Boyhood and Youth*, p. 89; Bade, *Steep Trails*, p. 12.

38. Henry Fairfield Osborn, "John Muir," *Sierra Club Bulletin* 10 (January 1916): 31.

39. Bade, *Steep Trails*, p. 18.

40. Henry Meade Bland, "John Muir," *Overland Monthly* 47 (June/July 1906): 522.

CHAPTER ONE

✳

HERBIVORES
("Dainty Feeders")

Most of John Muir's wildlife writings featured herbivores. Turn-of-the-century readers responded enthusiastically to his sunny portrayals of sheep, deer, and rodents. The last essay in this section, however, demonstrates Muir's awareness of the darker side of animal life. Although he often denied the natural world's brutality, Muir was too astute an observer to overlook death entirely.

Through these portrayals, Muir intended to convert his readers' affection for his subjects into an active concern for their welfare. While he devoted much attention to "safe," inoffensive animals, a strong conservationist message emerged from Muir's writings. Humans, he claimed in "The Wild Sheep of California," are "the unsatisfiable enemy of all nature." The following essays encourage readers to view animals from a broad, unselfish perspective.

The Wild Sheep
of California

NEARLY ALL OF THE LOFTY MOUNTAIN
chains of the globe are inhabited by wild sheep, which are
ordinarily classified under five or six distinct species.
These are the argali (*Ovis ammon*, Lin.), found throughout all the principal mountains of Asia; the burrhal (*Ov.
burrhel*), of the upper Himalayas; the Corsican wild sheep
(*Ov. musimon*, Pal.); the African (*Ov. tragelephus*, Cuv.);
and the American bighorn (*Ov. montana*, Cuv.). This last,
also called the Rocky Mountain sheep, is identical with the
wild sheep of the Sierra Nevada. Its range, according to
Professor Baird, extends from the region of the upper
Missouri and Yellowstone to the Rocky Mountains and the
high grounds adjacent to them on the eastern slope, and as
far south as the Rio Grande. Westward they extend as far as

5

❋ Herbivores ❋

the Cascade and Coast ranges of Washington, Oregon, and California, and follow the highlands some distance into Mexico.*

In California, the wild sheep ranks among the noblest of animal mountaineers. Possessed of keen sight, immovable nerve, and strong limbs, he dwells secure amid the loftiest summits of the Sierra, leaping unscathed from crag to crag, crossing foaming torrents and slopes of frozen snow, exposed to the wildest storms, yet maintaining a brave life, and developing from generation to generation in perfect strength and beauty. Compared with the argali, which, considering its size and the vast extent of its range, is perhaps the most important of all the wild sheep, the horns of our species are more regularly curved and less divergent at the base and near the tips; moreover, the argali may not be quite so large, but their more important characters are essentially the same, some of the best naturalists maintaining that they are only varied forms of one species. Cuvier conjectures that the argali may have come to this continent by crossing Behring's Straits on the ice.

It is generally supposed that the innumerable breeds of domestic sheep have been derived from the various wild species, but the whole question is involved in obscurity. According to Darwin, sheep have been domesticated from a very ancient period, the remains of a small breed differing from any now known having been found in the famous Swiss lake-dwellings. Compared with the best known domestic breeds, we find that our wild species is two or three

*Pacific Railroad Survey, vol. viii., page 678.

times as large, full-grown specimens weighing from 200 to 350 pounds. Instead of wool, they are covered with a thick mattress of coarse hair, like that of the deer, with only a very little fine wool at the bottom; but, though coarse, this hair is soft and spongy, and lies smoothly, as if carefully tended with comb and brush. I have frequently observed some of the same kind of coarse hair mixed with the wool of Mexican sheep. The predominant color is brownish gray, varying somewhat with the seasons; the belly and a large conspicuous patch on the buttocks are white, and the tail, which is very short, is black, with a yellowish border. The horns of the male are of immense size, measuring in their greater diameter from five to six inches, and in length around the curve from two to three feet. They are yellowish white in color, and ridged transversely, like those of the domestic ram. Their cross-section near the base is somewhat triangular in outline. In rising from the head they curve gently backward and outward, then forward and outward, until about three-fourths of a circle has been described, and until the tips, which are flattened and blunt, are about two feet apart. Two specimens found last summer on the head-waters of the San Joaquin measured as follows: Circumference at the base, 13½ and 16¼ inches; distance across from tip to tip, 22 and 24 inches. Those of the female are more flattened, less curved, and much smaller, measuring only six or seven inches in length along the curve. The following measurements of a male, obtained from the Rocky Mountains, are from Audubon:*

*Audubon and Bachman's *Quadrupeds of North America*.

7

* Herbivores *

	Ft.	In.
Length	6	0
Height at shoulder	3	5
Girth behind shoulders	3	11
Length of tail	0	5
Length of horns around curve	2	10½
Length of hair on back and sides	0	2 to 2½
Weight, 344 pounds.		

Besides these differences in size, color, and clothing, we might note that in form the domestic sheep is expressionless, like a round bundle of something only half alive; the wild is elegant as a deer, and every muscle glows with life. The tame is timid; the wild is bold. The tame is always ruffled and soiled; the wild is trim and clean as the flowers of its pasture.

The earliest mention that I have been able to find of our sheep, is by Father Picolo, a Catholic missionary at Monterey, in the year 1797, who, after describing it as being as large as a calf one or two years old, and as having the body of a deer with the head and horns of a sheep, adds, "I have eaten of these beasts; their flesh is very tender and delicious." Mackenzie mentions them in his travels as a kind of buffalo. A few of the more energetic of the Mono Indians hunt the sheep every season among the slate summits between Castle Peak and Mount Lyell, this section of the Sierra being comparatively easy of access, and here, from having been pursued, they are now extremely wary; but farther to the south, in the wilderness of snowy peaks,

8

where the many rugged branches of the San Joaquin and King's rivers take their rise, they fear no hunter save the wolf, and are more guileless and approachable than any of their tame kindred.

I have been greatly interested in studying their habits during the last four years, while engaged in the work of exploring these high regions. In spring and summer the males form separate bands. They are usually met in small flocks, numbering from three to twenty, feeding along the edges of glacier meadows, or resting among the castle-like crags of lofty summits; and, whether feeding or resting, or scaling wild cliffs for pleasure, their noble forms, the very embodiment of muscular beauty, never fail to strike the beholder with liveliest admiration. Their resting-places seem to be chosen with reference to sunshine and a wide outlook, and, most of all, to safety from the attacks of wolves. Their feeding-grounds are among the most beautiful of the wild Sierra gardens, bright with daisies and gentians, and mats of blooming shrubs. These are hidden away high on the sides of rough cañons, where light is abundant, or down in the valleys, along lake-borders, and stream-banks, where the plushy turf is greenest, and the purple heather grows. Sweet grasses also grow in these happy Alpine gardens, but the wild sheep eats little besides the spicy leaves and shoots of the various shrubs and bushes, perhaps relishing both their taste and beauty, although tame men are slow to suspect wild sheep of seeing more than grass. When winter storms fall, decking their summer pastures in the lavish bloom of snow, then, like the

* Herbivores *

blue-birds and robins, our brave sheep gather and go to warmer climates, usually descending the eastern flank of the range to the narrow, birch-filled gorges that open into the sage plains, where snow never falls to any great depth, the elevation above the sea being about from 5,000 to 7,000 feet. Here they sojourn until spring sunshine unlocks the cañons and warms the pastures of their glorious Alps.

In the months of June and July they bring forth their young, in the most solitary and inaccessible crags, far above the nest of the eagle. I have frequently come upon the beds of the ewes and lambs at an elevation of from 12,000 to 13,000 feet above sea-level. These beds consist simply of an oval-shaped hollow, pawed out among loose disintegrating rock-chips and sand, upon some sunny spot commanding a good outlook, and partially sheltered from the winds that sweep passionately across those lofty crags almost without intermission. Such is the cradle of the little mountaineer, aloft in the sky, rocked in storms, curtained in clouds, sleeping in thin, icy air; but wrapped in his hairy coat, nourished by a warm, strong mother, defended from the talons of the eagle and teeth of the sly coyote, the bonnie lamb grows apace. He learns to nibble the purple daisy and leaves of the white spiræa; his horns begin to shoot, and ere summer is done, he is strong and agile, and goes forth with the flock, shepherded by the same Divine love that tends the more helpless human lamb in its warm cradle by the fireside.

Like the Alp-climbing ibex of Europe, our mountain-

eer is said to plunge fearlessly down the faces of sheer precipices, and alight on his huge elastic horns. I know only
two hunters who claim to have witnessed this feat; I never
was so fortunate. They describe the act as a diving head-
foremost. Some of the horns that I have examined with
reference to this question are certainly much battered in
front, and are so large at the base that they cover all the
upper portion of the head down nearly to a level with the
eyes; moreover, the skull of a wild sheep is stronger than a
bull's. I struck an old bleached specimen on Mount Ritter
a dozen blows with my ice-axe without breaking it. Such
skulls would not fracture very readily by the wildest rock-
diving; but other bones might, and the numerous mechan-
ical difficulties in the way of controlling the movements of
their bodies after striking upon an irregular rock-surface
would seem to make such a bowlder-like method of progression improbable, even for the big-horned rams, much
more for the ewes. Perhaps when a great leap is made they
may endeavor to lighten the shock upon their legs, and
assist in arresting farther progress, by striking their horns
against any rock that may chance to be favorably situated
for the purpose, just as men mountaineers do with their
hands.

Nothing is more commonly remarked by travelers in the
high Sierra than the absence of animal life; but if such
would go singly, without haste or noise, away from the
region of trails and pack-trains, they would speedily learn
that these mountain mansions are not without inhabitants,
many of whom, confiding and gentle, would be glad to

make their acquaintance. Last September, I was following the south fork of the San Joaquin up its wild cañon to its farthest icy fountains. It was the season of mountain Indian summer. The sun beamed lovingly, squirrels were nutting amid the pinecones, butterflies hovered about the last of the golden-rods, willow and maple groves were yellow, the meadows were brown, and the whole mellow landscape glowed like a countenance with the deepest and sweetest repose. On my way along the rocky river-side, I came to a fine meadowy expansion of the cañon, about two miles long and half a mile wide, inclosed with picturesque granite walls like those of Yosemite, and with the river sweeping through its groves and meadows in magnificent curves. This little Yosemite was full of wild life. Deer with their fawns constantly bounded from thicket to thicket as I advanced. Grouse kept rising from the brown grass with a great whirring of wings, and, alighting on low branches of the poplar or pine, allowed a near approach, as if pleased to be observed. A broad-shouldered wild-cat showed himself, coming out of a grove and crossing the river upon a flood-jam of logs. The bird-like tamias frisked about among pine-needles and seedy grass-tufts. Cranes waded the shallows of the river bends, the kingfisher rattled from perch to perch, and the blessed ousel sung with the leaping spray of every cascade. Purple evening came as I lingered in the company of these mountain dwellers, and, as darkness fell, I awoke from their enchantment and sought a camping-spot near the river. I slept among the yellow leaves of an aspen grove, and, pushing forward next morning, discovered yet grander landscapes and grander life. The scenery became more Alpine. The lofty sugar-pine and silver fir gave place to the hardier cedar and dwarf pine, the cañon walls became more jagged and bare, and gentians became more abundant in the gardens of the river bank. In the afternoon, I came to a valley strikingly wild in all its features. As regards area of bottom, it is one of the very smallest of San Joaquin Yosemites; but its walls are sublime, rising from 2,000 to 4,000 feet above the river. At the head of the valley, the river forks, as is found to be the case in all Yosemites. Its formation was accomplished by the action of two vast ice-rivers, whose fountains were on the flanks of mounts Humphreys and Emerson, and mountains farther south. On their recession at the close of the great winter, this valley basin became first a lake; then a sedgy meadow; then, filled with flood-bowlders and logs, and planted with bushes and grass, it became the Yosemite of to-day—a range for wild sheep, whose tracks I saw printed everywhere along its briery lanes and gulches.

The chafed river sings loud on its way down the valley, but above its deafening songs I could hear the heavier booming of a water-fall, which caused me to push eagerly forward. Emerging from the tangled groves at the head of the valley, I beheld the young San Joaquin coming from its fountains in a glorious cascade. Scanning the steep incline down which the white waters thundered, I discovered a crooked seam, by which I climbed to the edge of a narrow terrace, which, crossing the cañon, divides the cascades nearly in the middle. Here I sat down to take breath and to make some entries in my note-book, taking advantage of my elevated position to gaze back down over the valley into the heart of the glorious landscape, little knowing the while what neighbors were near. Chancing to look across the cascade, there stood three wild sheep within a few yards, calmly observing me. Never did the sudden appearance of human friend, or mountain, or waterfall, so forcibly seize and rivet my attention. Anxiety to observe accurately on so rare an opportunity checked enthusiasm. Eagerly I marked the flowing undulations of their firm-braided limbs; their strong, straight legs, size, color, ears, eyes, heads; their graceful rounded necks, the upsweeping cycloidal curve of their noble horns. When they moved, I devoured every gesture; while they, in nowise disconcerted either by my attention or by the loud roar of the waters, advanced slowly up the rapids, often turning to look at me. Presently, they made a dash at a steep ice-polished incline, and reached the top without a struggle, by a succession of short, stiff leaps, bringing their hoofs down sharply with a patting sound. This was the most astounding feat of mountaineering I had ever witnessed. Just a few days previous, my cautious, iron-shod mules fell, on good rough ground, descending the cañon-side in lawless avalanche; and many a time I have been compelled to tie my shoes and stockings to my belt, and creep up far easier slopes with the utmost caution. No wonder, then, I watched the progress of these animal mountaineers with intensest sympathy, and exulted in the boundless sufficiency of wild nature displayed in their invention, construction, and keeping. But judge the measure of my overjoy when, a few moments later, I caught sight of a dozen more in one flock near the base of the upper cascade. They were on the same side of the river with me, distant only twenty-five or thirty yards, and looking as unworn, calm, and bright, as if created on the spot. It appears that when I came up the cañon, they all were feeding together in the valley, and in their haste to reach high ground, where they could look about them to ascertain the nature of the disturbance, they were divided, three having ascended on one side of the cascade, the rest on the other. The main flock, headed by an experienced chief, began to cross the rapids soon after I first observed them. The crossing of swift torrents on chance bowlders is nerve-trying work even for men mountaineers, yet these shepherdless sheep leaped from bowlder to bowlder, and held themselves in perfect poise above the whirling current, as if doing nothing extraordinary. The immediate foreground of the rare picture before me, was glossy ice-planed granite, traversed by seams in which grew rock-ferns and tufts of heathy bryanthus, the gray cañon walls on both sides splendidly sculptured, and adorned with brown cedars and pines; in the distance, lofty mountains rising far into the thin blue sky; in the centre, the snowy cascade, the voice and the soul of all, fringing shrubs waving time to its thunder-tones; and in front, the brave sheep, their gray forms slightly obscured in the spray, yet firmly defined on the close, dense white of the cataract, their huge rough horns

rising in the midst like upturned roots of dead pine-trees—
the setting sun lighting the cañon, purpling and glorifying
all.

After crossing the river, the dauntless climbers, led by
their chief, at once began to scale the cañon wall; now right,
now left, in long single file, leaping in succession from cliff
to cliff; now ascending slippery dome-curves; now walking
the edges of precipices, stopping at times to gaze down at
me from some flat-topped rock, with heads held aslant, as
if curious to find out whether I was about to follow. When
they had reached the top of the wall, 1,500 to 2,000 feet
high, I could still see their noble forms outlined on the sky
as they lingered, looking down in groups of two or three,
giving rare animation to the sublime cliffs. Throughout
the whole ascent, I did not observe a single awkward step
or unsuccessful effort. I have often seen tame sheep in the
mountains jump upon a sloping rock-surface, hold on
tremulously a few seconds, and fall back baffled and irre-
solute; but in the most trying dangers, where the slightest
inaccuracy would have resulted in destruction, these
moved with magnificent reliance on their strength and
skill, the limits of which they never seemed to know.

Moreover, each one of the flock, though acknowledging
the right of leadership to the most experienced, climbed
with intelligent independence—a perfect individual, capable of separate existence whenever it should choose to
secede from the little clan. But the domestic sheep is only a
fraction of an animal, a whole flock being required to form
an individual, just as numerous florets are required for the

making of one complete sunflower. Shepherds acquainted with mountain dangers, who in watching by night and day have beheld their feeble flocks broken by bears, crushed and disintegrated by storms, and scattered diverse in the rocks like wind-driven chaff, will in some measure appreciate the strong self-reliance and noble individuality of nature's sheep.

The only animal which may fairly be regarded as a companion of our sheep, is the so-called Rocky Mountain goat (*Aplocerus montanus*, Rich), which according to Professor Baird is far more antelope than goat. He, too, is a brave and hardy fellow, fearlessly accompanying our sheep on the wildest summits, and braving with him the severest storms, but smaller and much less dignified in demeanor, and the long white hair with which his body is covered obscures the expression of his limbs. His jet-black horns are only about five or six inches long. I have never seen this American chamois, although a few small flocks have been found in the Sierra. In some portions of the Rocky and Cascade ranges it is said to occur in flocks of considerable size, where it is hunted by the Indians, who make use of its skin in various ways, that of the head with the horns attached being sometimes worn as a cap.

Three species of deer occur in California—the black-tailed, white-tailed, and mule-deer. The first-mentioned species (*Cervus columbianus*) is by far the most common, and is frequently met by our sheep in summer on high glacier meadows, and along the outskirts of the upper forests; but being a forest animal, seeking shelter, and rearing its young in dense thickets, it seldom visits our sheep in his higher homes. The antelope, though not a mountaineer, is occasionally met during his winter sojourn on the edge of the sage-plains. The elk (*Cervus canadensis*) still exists in a few places along the base of the Sierra, but I doubt if our sheep has ever seen him.

Perhaps no animal in the world is without its enemy, but mountaineers as a class have fewer enemies than lowlanders. Our Sierra sheep seems to be favored above his companions. The panther pounces upon the antelope and deer, but his track is seldom seen crossing the craggy threshold of the sheep, nor is he often exposed to the hunter's rifle. A few perish by swift and heavy snow-storms. Two that I found last summer on the side of a glacial meadow, appear to have perished in this way; and three were discovered snow-bound in Bloody Cañon, a few years ago, and killed with an axe by some men who had occasion to cross the range by the Mono Pass, in midwinter. The bear can hardly be considered an enemy, for though sometimes he leaves berries and acorns for mutton, he prefers hunting the tame and helpless civilized sheep. The eagle and coyote occasionally capture an unprotected lamb, or some unfortunate herd beset in deep snow; but these are little more than accidents, and as for man, the unsatisfiable enemy of all nature, our sheep have little to fear from him, because, like stars and angels, they dwell mostly above his reach in the sky. The golden plains of Sacramento and San Joaquin were recently thronged with bands of antelope, but being fertile and accessible they are required for human pastures;

✻ The Wild Sheep of California ✻

so also are the splendid feeding-grounds of the deer—hill, valley, forest, and meadow; but it will be long ere he will be able to take and use the highland castles of the sheep; and remembering here how rapidly whole species of the noble animals are disappearing before the footsteps of man, all lovers of wilderness life will rejoice with me in the rocky security of *Ovis montana*, the bravest mountaineer of the Sierra.

Deer

THE SIERRA DEER — THE BLACKTAIL —
spend the winters in the brushy and exceedingly rough region just below the main timber-belt, and are less accessible to hunters there than when they are passing through the
comparatively open forests to and from their summer pastures near the summits of the range. They go up the mountains early in the spring as the snow melts, not waiting for
it all to disappear; reaching the high Sierra about the first
of June, and the coolest recesses at the base of the peaks a
month or so later. I have tracked them for miles over com-
pacted snow from three to ten feet deep.

Deer are capital mountaineers, making their way into
the heart of the roughest mountains; seeking not only pasturage, but a cool climate, and safe hidden places in which
to bring forth their young. They are not supreme as rock-

climbing animals; they take second rank, yielding the first
to the mountain sheep, which dwell above them on the
highest crags and peaks. Still, the two meet frequently; for
the deer climbs all the peaks save the lofty summits above
the glaciers, crossing piles of angular boulders, roaring
swollen streams, and sheer-walled cañons by fords and
passes that would try the nerves of the hardiest mountaineers,—climbing with graceful ease and reserve of strength
that cannot fail to arouse admiration. Everywhere some
species of deer seems to be at home,—on rough or smooth
ground, lowlands or highlands, in swamps and barrens
and the densest woods, in varying climates, hot or cold,
over all the continent; maintaining glorious health, never
making an awkward step. Standing, lying down, walking,
feeding, running even for life, it is always invincibly
graceful, and adds beauty and animation to every landscape,—a charming animal, and a great credit to nature.

I never see one of the common blacktail deer, the only
species in the Park, without fresh admiration; and since I
never carry a gun I see them well: lying beneath a juniper
or dwarf pine, among the brown needles on the brink of
some cliff or the end of a ridge commanding a wide outlook; feeding in sunny openings among chaparral, daintily
selecting aromatic leaves and twigs; leading their fawns out
of my way, or making them lie down and hide; bounding
past through the forest, or curiously advancing and retreat-
ing again and again.

One morning when I was eating breakfast in a little garden spot on the Kaweah, hedged around with chaparral, I

* Herbivores *

noticed a deer's head thrust through the bushes, the big beautiful eyes gazing at me. I kept still, and the deer ventured forward a step, then snorted and withdrew. In a few minutes she returned, and came into the open garden, stepping with infinite grace, followed by two others. After showing themselves for a moment, they bounded over the hedge with sharp, timid snorts and vanished. But curiosity brought them back with still another, and all four came into my garden, and, satisfied that I meant them no ill, began to feed, actually eating breakfast with me, like tame, gentle sheep around a shepherd,—rare company, and the most graceful in movements and attitudes. I eagerly watched them while they fed on ceanothus and wild cherry, daintily culling single leaves here and there from the side of the hedge, turning now and then to snip a few leaves of mint from the midst of the garden flowers. Grass they did not eat at all. No wonder the contents of the deer's stomach are eaten by the Indians.

While exploring the upper cañon of the north fork of the San Joaquin, one evening, the sky threatening rain, I searched for a dry bed, and made choice of a big juniper that had been pushed down by a snow avalanche, but was resting stubbornly on its knees high enough to let me lie under its broad trunk. Just below my shelter there was another juniper on the very brink of a precipice, and, examining it, I found a deer-bed beneath it, completely protected and concealed by drooping branches,—a fine refuge and lookout as well as resting-place. About an hour before dark I heard the clear, sharp snorting of a deer, and looking down on the brushy, rocky cañon bottom, discovered an anxious doe that no doubt had her fawns concealed near by. She bounded over the chaparral and up the farther slope of the wall, often stopping to look back and listen,—a fine picture of vivid, eager alertness. I sat perfectly still, and as my shirt was colored like the juniper bark I was not easily seen. After a little she came cautiously toward me, sniffing the air and grazing, and her movements, as she descended the cañon side over boulder piles and brush and fallen timber, were admirably strong and beautiful; she never strained or made apparent efforts, although jumping high here and there. As she drew nigh she sniffed anxiously, trying the air in different directions until she caught my scent; then bounded off, and vanished behind a small grove of firs. Soon she came back with the same caution and insatiable curiosity,—coming and going five or six times. While I sat admiring her, a Douglas squirrel, evidently excited by her noisy alarms, climbed a boulder beneath me, and witnessed her performances as attentively as I did, while a frisky chipmunk, too restless or hungry for such shows, busied himself about his supper in a thicket of shad-bushes, the fruit of which was then ripe, glancing about on the slender twigs lightly as a sparrow.

Toward the end of the Indian summer, when the young are strong, the deer begin to gather in little bands of from six to fifteen or twenty, and on the approach of the first snowstorm they set out on their march down the mountains to their winter quarters; lingering usually on warm hillsides and spurs eight or ten miles below the summits, as if loath to leave. About the end of November, a heavy, far-reaching storm drives them down in haste along the dividing ridges between the rivers, led by old experienced bucks whose knowledge of the topography is wonderful.

It is when the deer are coming down that the Indians set out on their grand fall hunt. Too lazy to go into the recesses of the mountains away from trails, they wait for the deer to come out, and then waylay them. This plan also has the advantage of finding them in bands. Great preparations are made. Old guns are mended, bullets moulded, and the hunters wash themselves and fast to some extent, to insure good luck, as they say. Men and women, old and young, set forth together. Central camps are made on the well-known highways of the deer, which are soon red with blood. Each hunter comes in laden, old crones as well as maidens smiling on the luckiest. All grow fat and merry. Boys, each armed with an antlered head, play at buck-fighting, and plague the industrious women, who are busily preparing the meat for transportation, by stealing up behind them and throwing fresh hides over them. But the Indians are passing away here as everywhere, and their red camps on the mountains are fewer every year.

Rodents

THE TWO SQUIRRELS OF THE PARK, THE Douglas and the California gray, keep all the woods lively. The former is far more abundant and more widely distributed, being found all the way up from the foothills to the dwarf pines on the Summit peaks. He is the most influential of the Sierra animals, though small, and the brightest of all the squirrels I know,—a squirrel of squirrels, quick mountain vigor and valor condensed, purely wild, and as free from disease as a sunbeam. One cannot think of such an animal ever being weary or sick. He claims all the woods, and is inclined to drive away even men as intruders. How he scolds, and what faces he makes! If not so comically small he would be a dreadful fellow. The gray, Sciurus fossor, is the handsomest, I think, of all the large American squirrels. He is something like the Eastern gray, but is brighter and clearer in color, and more lithe and slender. He dwells in the oak and pine woods up to a height of about five thousand feet above the sea, is rather common in Yosemite Valley, Hetch-Hetchy, Kings River Cañon, and indeed in all the main cañons and Yosemites, but does not like the high fir-covered ridges. Compared with the Douglas, the gray is more than twice as large; nevertheless, he manages to make his way through the trees with less stir than his small, peppery neighbor, and is much less influential in every way. In the spring, before the pine-nuts and hazelnuts are ripe, he examines last year's cones for the few seeds that may be left in them between the half-open scales, and gleans fallen nuts and seeds on the ground among the leaves, after making sure that no enemy is nigh. His fine tail floats, now behind, now above him, level or gracefully curled, light and radiant as dry thistledown. His body seems hardly more substantial than his tail. The Douglas is a firm, emphatic bolt of life, fiery, pungent, full of brag and show and fight, and his movements have none of the elegant deliberation of the gray. They are so quick and keen they almost sting the onlooker, and the acrobatic harlequin gyrating show he makes of himself turns one giddy to see. The gray is shy and oftentimes stealthy, as if half expecting to find an enemy in every tree and bush and behind every log; he seems to wish to be let alone, and manifests no desire to be seen, or admired, or feared. He is hunted by the Indians, and this of itself is cause enough for caution. The Douglas is less attractive for game, and probably increasing in numbers in spite of every enemy. He goes his ways bold as a lion, up and down and across, round and round, the happiest, merriest of all the hairy tribe, and at the same time tremendously earnest and solemn, sunshine incarnate, making every tree tingle with his electric toes. If you prick him, you cannot think he will bleed. He seems above the chance and change that beset common mortals, though in busily gathering burs and nuts he shows that he has to work for a living, like the rest of us. I never found a dead Douglas. He gets into the world and out of it without being noticed; only in prime is he seen, like some little plants that are visible only when in bloom.

The little striped Tamias quadrivittatus is one of the most amiable and delightful of all the mountain tree-climbers. A brighter, cheerier chipmunk does not exist. He is smarter, more arboreal and squirrel-like, than the familiar Eastern species, and is distributed as widely on the Sierra as the Douglas. Every forest, however dense or open, every hilltop and cañon, however brushy or bare, is cheered and enlivened by this happy little animal. You are likely to notice him first on the lower edge of the coniferous belt, where the Sabine and yellow pines meet; and thence upward, go where you may, you will find him every day, even in winter, unless the weather is stormy. He is an exceedingly interesting little fellow, full of odd, quaint ways, confiding, thinking no evil; and without being a squirrel—a true shadow-tail—he lives the life of a squirrel, and has almost all squirrelish accomplishments without aggressive quarrelsomeness.

I never weary of watching him as he frisks about the

bushes, gathering seeds and berries; poising on slender twigs of wild cherry, shad, chinquapin, buckthorn, bramble; skimming along prostrate trunks or over the grassy, needle-strewn forest floor; darting from boulder to boulder on glacial pavements and the tops of the great domes. When the seeds of the conifers are ripe, he climbs the trees and cuts off the cones for a winter store, working diligently, though not with the tremendous lightning energy of the Douglas, who frequently drives him out of the best trees. Then he lies in wait, and picks up a share of the burs cut off by his domineering cousin, and stores them beneath logs and in hollows. Few of the Sierra animals are so well liked as this little airy, fluffy half squirrel, half spermophile. So gentle, confiding, and busily cheery and happy, he takes one's heart and keeps his place among the best-loved of the mountain darlings. A diligent collector of seeds, nuts, and berries, of course he is well fed, though never in the least dumpy with fat. On the contrary, he looks like a mere fluff of fur, weighing but little more than a field mouse, and of his frisky, birdlike liveliness without haste there is no end. Douglas can bark with his mouth closed, but little quad always opens his when he talks or sings. He has a considerable variety of notes which correspond with his movements, some of them sweet and liquid, like water dripping into a pool with tinkling sound. His eyes are black and animated, shining like dew. He seems dearly to like teasing a dog, venturing within a few feet of it, then frisking away with a lively chipping and low squirrelish churring; beating time to his music, such as it is, with his tail, which at

each chip and churr describes a half circle. Not even Douglas is surer footed or takes greater risks. I have seen him
running about on sheer Yosemite cliffs, holding on with as
little effort as a fly and as little thought of danger, in places
where, if he had made the least slip, he would have fallen
thousands of feet. How fine it would be could mountaineers move about on precipices with the same sure grip!

Before the pine-nuts are ripe, grass seeds and those of
the many species of ceanothus, with strawberries, raspberries, and the soft red thimbleberries of Rubus nutkanus,
form the bulk of his food, and a neater eater is not to be
found in the mountains. Bees powdered with pollen, poking their blunt noses into the bells of flowers, are comparatively clumsy and boorish. Frisking along some fallen
pine or fir, when the grass seeds are ripe, he looks about
him, considering which of the tufts he sees is likely to have
the best, runs out to it, selects what he thinks is sure to be a
good head, cuts it off, carries it to the top of the log, sits
upright and nibbles out the grain without getting awns in
his mouth, turning the head round, holding it and finger-
ing it as if playing on a flute; then skips for another and
another, bringing them to the same dining-log.

The woodchuck (*Arctomys monax*) dwells on high bleak
ridges and boulder piles; and a very different sort of mountaineer is he,—bulky, fat, aldermanic, and fairly bloated
at times by hearty indulgence in the lush pastures of his
airy home. And yet he is by no means a dull animal. In the
midst of what we regard as storm-beaten desolation, high
in the frosty air, beside the glaciers he pipes and whistles

right cheerily and lives to a good old age. If you are as early a riser as he is, you may oftentimes see him come blinking out of his burrow to meet the first beams of the morning and take a sunbath on some favorite flat-topped boulder. Afterward, well warmed, he goes to breakfast in one of his garden hollows, eats heartily like a cow in clover until comfortably swollen, then goes a-visiting, and plays and loves and fights.

In the spring of 1875, when I was exploring the peaks and glaciers about the head of the middle fork of the San Joaquin, I had crossed the range from the head of Owen River, and one morning, passing around a frozen lake where the snow was perhaps ten feet deep, I was surprised to find the fresh track of a woodchuck plainly marked, the sun having softened the surface. What could the animal be thinking of, coming out so early while all the ground was snow-buried? The steady trend of his track showed he had a definite aim, and fortunately it was toward a mountain thirteen thousand feet high that I meant to climb. So I followed to see if I could find out what he was up to. From the base of the mountain the track pointed straight up, and I knew by the melting snow that I was not far behind him. I lost the track on a crumbling ridge, partly projecting through the snow, but soon discovered it again. Well toward the summit of the mountain, in an open spot on the south side, nearly inclosed by disintegrating pinnacles among which the sun heat reverberated, making an isolated patch of warm climate, I found a nice garden, full of rock cress, phlox, silene, draba, etc., and a few grasses;

and in this garden I overtook the wanderer, enjoying a fine fresh meal, perhaps the first of the season. How did he know the way to this one garden spot, so high and far off, and what told him that it was in bloom while yet the snow was ten feet deep over his den? For this it would seem he would need more botanical, topographical, and climatological knowledge than most mountaineers are possessed of.

The shy, curious mountain beaver, Haplodon, lives on the heights, not far from the woodchuck. He digs canals and controls the flow of small streams under the sod. And it is startling when one is camped on the edge of a sloping meadow near the homes of these industrious mountaineers, to be awakened in the still night by the sound of water rushing and gurgling under one's head in a newly formed canal. Pouched gophers always have a way of awakening nervous campers that is quite as exciting as the Haplodon's plan; that is, by a series of firm upward pushes when they are driving tunnels and shoving up the dirt. One naturally cries out, "Who's there?" and then discovering the cause, "All right. Go on. Good-night," and goes to sleep again.

The haymaking pika, bob-tailed spermophile, and wood-rat are also among the most interesting of the Sierra animals. The last, Neotoma, is scarcely at all like the common rat, is nearly twice as large, has a delicate, soft, brownish fur, white on the belly, large ears thin and translucent, eyes full and liquid and mild in expression, nose blunt and squirrelish, slender claws sharp as needles, and as his limbs are strong he can climb about as well as a squirrel; while no rat or squirrel has so innocent a look, is so easily approached, or in general expresses so much confidence in one's good intentions. He seems too fine for the thorny thickets he inhabits, and his big, rough hut is as unlike himself as possible. No other animal in these mountains makes nests so large and striking in appearance as his. They are built of all kinds of sticks (broken branches, and old rotten moss-grown chunks and green twigs, smooth or thorny, cut from the nearest bushes), mixed with miscellaneous rubbish and curious odds and ends,—bits of cloddy earth, stones, bones, bits of deer-horn, etc.: the whole simply piled in conical masses on the ground in chaparral thickets. Some of these cabins are five or six feet high, and occasionally a dozen or more are grouped together; less, perhaps, for society's sake than for advantages of food and shelter.

Coming through deep, stiff chaparral in the heart of the wilderness, heated and weary in forcing a way, the solitary explorer, happening into one of these curious neotoma villages, is startled at the strange sight, and may imagine he is in an Indian village, and feel anxious as to the reception he will get in a place so wild. At first, perhaps, not a single inhabitant will be seen, or at most only two or three seated on the tops of their huts as at the doors, observing the stranger with the mildest of mild eyes. The nest in the centre of the cabin is made of grass and films of bark chewed to tow, and lined with feathers and the down of various seeds. The thick, rough walls seem to be built for defense against enemies—fox, coyote, etc.—as well as for shelter, and the delicate creatures in their big, rude homes, suggest tender flowers, like those of Salvia carduacea, defended by thorny involucres.

Sometimes the home is built in the forks of an oak, twenty or thirty feet from the ground, and even in garrets. Among housekeepers who have these bushmen as neighbors or guests they are regarded as thieves, because they carry away and pile together everything transportable (knives, forks, tin cups, spoons, spectacles, combs, nails, kindling-wood, etc., as well as eatables of all sorts), to strengthen their fortifications or to shine among rivals. Once, far back in the high Sierra, they stole my snowgoggles, the lid of my teapot, and my aneroid barometer; and one stormy night, when encamped under a prostrate cedar, I was awakened by a gritting sound on the granite, and by the light of my fire I discovered a handsome neotoma beside me, dragging away my ice-hatchet, pulling with might and main by a buckskin string on the handle. I threw bits of bark at him and made a noise to frighten him, but he stood scolding and chattering back at me, his fine eyes shining with an air of injured innocence.

The Porcupine

THE PORCUPINE IS A SLOW-GOING CON-
tented-looking animal offering no harm to anybody that
lets him alone. I never knew a porcupine to bring on a
quarrel. They always try to live quietly and inoffensively
with all their neighbors, including man. They are very
slow of foot and when running as fast as they can their speed
is little more than a fast walk for a man. The porcupine is
nearly always found in summer hiding beneath fallen trees
well up in the mountains, usually at an elevation of about
seven thousand to ten thousand feet. His food, as far as I
have been able to ascertain, is chiefly the twigs and bark of
willows and pines—generally the two-leaved pine. He is a
pretty good swimmer, not afraid to enter ice-cold water,
nor afraid to travel on thick snow and glaciers. Dogs frequently attack them, but when they try to close in, the por-

✳ The Porcupine ✳

cupine strikes viciously with his tail, which is bristling with barbed spines, and should the dog close in he gets a mouthful of spears, no matter what part of the body he bites, for they are covered all over with the quills. Dogs suffer cruelly from these barbed spines which have to be extracted with forceps before the poor dog is able to eat.

Two young naturalists were collecting specimens of mammals on the edge of the timber line to the south of the Tuolumne meadows opposite the Soda Springs, and as usual with boys coming into the high mountains they had good appetites. They loaded the mule with provisions at the main camp, but very soon made their appearance again, and in another day or two came back, having used all the flour, and especially all the bacon which was supposed to last for a week or two. When asked what in the world they had done with all the bacon they took with them, they said they had eaten it but that they did not come down when they first found themselves out of bacon, but now they had to come because their appetites were so good. They continued making their appearance with the mule for another load of bacon and flour as they kept getting hungrier and hungrier at shorter and shorter intervals, but since they were again so closely questioned as to what they were doing with the bacon they became ashamed to come until compelled to, so they began to test the flesh of all the mammals they trapped on the timber line. After skinning them they ate the flesh. They had heard that frogs were good to eat, and as their camp stood near a little glacier lake in which the frogs were merrily singing, they carefully began to hunt frogs until they had nearly exterminated them from that pond. One night when they were feeling that they must go down for more provisions, no matter what the head naturalist thought of them, they saw a dark-looking object walking on a snow bank well up above the timber line. Hunger made them think of eating everything that moved so they immediately ran toward the object thinking it might be good to eat. This proved to be a porcupine, and not having guns with them, they brutally murdered it by blows with their heavy boots. As they complained of the cold at that high altitude they slept in winter with their clothing on and also their boots and leggings, and while they were fighting the poor porcupine, who was defending himself with his tail, they found, after having killed him, that each of them had many of these barbed spines driven through their leather leggings and their clothes. They skinned the porcupine and the fat plump body assuaged in a measure their pangs of hunger.

In the forests of this region, especially on the edges of open meadows where the porcupines feed in summer, a large percentage of the two-leaved pine are all but stripped of their bark to a great height. Quite a number are killed outright by being fairly girdled, while others are only half girdled but are stripped of the bark clear up to the branches. It seems that this hardy animal, when hungry, had only to go to the nearest tree, climb it and seat himself comfortably on a limb and eat, stripping off the entire bark, outside as well as inside. Whether the animal ascends the tree every time he is hungry, or whether he climbs the tree and remains in it until he has eaten all the bark I do not know. It looks as though that was his plan. Simply when he found a good tree to climb he stayed for weeks, although some, no doubt, winter under rocks that are comparatively warm from absorbed summer sun heat.

Animal Death

ONE CALM SUMMER EVENING A RED-
headed woodpecker was drowned in our lake.* The accident happened at the south end, opposite our memorable
swimming-hole, a few rods from the place where I came so
near being drowned years before. I had returned to the old
home during a summer vacation of the State University,
and, having made a beginning in botany, I was, of course,
full of enthusiasm and ran eagerly to my beloved pogonia,
calopogon, and cypripedium gardens, osmunda ferneries,
and the lake lilies and pitcher-plants. A little before sundown the day-breeze died away, and the lake, reflecting the
wooded hills like a mirror, was dimpled and dotted and
streaked here and there where fishes and turtles were pok-

*Muir spent his late childhood on his family's Wisconsin farm near Fountain
Lake (now called Ennis Lake).

38

ing out their heads and muskrats were sculling themselves along with their flat tails making glittering tracks. After lingering awhile, dreamily recalling the old, hard, half-happy days, and watching my favorite red-headed woodpeckers pursuing moths like regular flycatchers, I swam out through the rushes and up the middle of the lake to the north end and back, gliding slowly, looking about me, enjoying the scenery as I would in a saunter along the shore, and studying the habits of the animals as they were explained and recorded on the smooth glassy water.

On the way back, when I was within a hundred rods or so of the end of my voyage, I noticed a peculiar plashing disturbance that could not, I thought, be made by a jumping fish or any other inhabitant of the lake; for instead of low regular out-circling ripples such as are made by the popping up of a head, or like those raised by the quick splash of a leaping fish, or diving loon or muskrat, a continuous struggle was kept up for several minutes ere the outspreading, interfering ring-waves began to die away. Swimming hastily to the spot to try to discover what had happened, I found one of my woodpeckers floating motionless with outspread wings. All was over. Had I been a minute or two earlier, I might have saved him. He had glanced on the water I suppose in pursuit of a moth, was unable to rise from it, and died struggling, as I nearly did at this same spot. Like me he seemed to have lost his mind in blind confusion and fear. The water was warm, and had he kept still with his head a little above the surface, he would sooner or later have been wafted ashore. The best aimed flights of birds and man "gang aft agley," but this was the first case I had witnessed of a bird losing its life by drowning.

Doubtless accidents to animals are far more common than is generally known. I have seen quails killed by flying against our house when suddenly startled. Some birds get entangled in hairs of their own nests and die. Once I found a poor snipe in our meadow that was unable to fly on account of difficult egg-birth. Pitying the poor mother, I picked her up out of the grass and helped her as gently as I could, and as soon as the egg was born she flew gladly away. Oftentimes I have thought it strange that one could walk through the woods and mountains and plains for years without seeing a single blood-spot. Most wild animals get into the world and out of it without being noticed. Nevertheless we at last sadly learn that they are all subject to the vicissitudes of fortune like ourselves. Many birds lose their lives in storms. I remember a particularly severe Wisconsin winter, when the temperature was many degrees below zero and the snow was deep, preventing the quail, which feed on the ground, from getting anything like enough food, as was pitifully shown by a flock I found on our farm frozen solid in a thicket of oak sprouts. They were in a circle about a foot wide, with their heads outward, packed close together for warmth. Yet all had died without a struggle, perhaps more from starvation than frost. Many small birds lose their lives in the storms of early spring, or even summer. One mild spring morning I picked up more than a score out of the grass and flowers, most of them darling singers that had perished in a sudden storm of sleety rain and hail.

In a hollow at the foot of an oak tree that I had chopped down one cold winter day, I found a poor ground squirrel frozen solid in its snug grassy nest, in the middle of a store of nearly a peck of wheat it had carefully gathered. I carried it home and gradually thawed and warmed it in the kitchen, hoping it would come to life like a pickerel I caught in our lake through a hole in the ice, which, after being frozen as hard as a bone and thawed at the fireside, squirmed itself out of the grasp of the cook when she began to scrape it, bounced off the table, and danced about on the floor, making wonderful springy jumps as if trying to find its way back home to the lake. But for the poor spermophile nothing I could do in the way of revival was of any avail. Its life had passed away without the slightest struggle, as it lay asleep curled up like a ball, with its tail wrapped about it.

CHAPTER TWO

*

BIRDS

Birds, claimed Frank M. Chapman, a curator at the American Museum of Natural History during John Muir's day, "are Nature's most vital and potent expressions." Indeed, the most popular topic of turn-of-the-century nature writing was amateur ornithology. Although John Burroughs, dubbed "John o' Birds," was best known in this genre, Muir, too, wrote bird essays. But his writings differed from those of Burroughs in his emphasis upon intelligence and individuality. Muir's descriptions offered more than mere physical details of species: he evoked the characters of his subjects. The water ouzel (his favorite), for instance, was commended for its irrepressible spirit, while the mountain quail—"the very handsomest and most interesting" of American partridges—was portrayed as being a particularly inquisitive bird.

Muir hoped, through his writings, to enlist sympathy for these creatures. He deplored the "shameful" slaughter of birds by humans; his observations on the once-abundant passenger pigeon are especially poignant, for in 1914, the year of his death, the last of this overhunted species died in the Cincinnati Zoological Garden.

Although he was not alone in his desire to protect birds, Muir, unlike his contemporaries, down-played their utilitarian value as consumers of noxious insects. To him, all animals had an in-trinsic worth apart from any usefulness to humans.

Among the Birds
of the Yosemite

TRAVELERS IN THE SIERRA FORESTS USU-
ally complain of the want of life. "The trees," they say, "are
fine, but the empty stillness is deadly; there are no animals
to be seen, no birds. We have not heard a song in all the
woods." And no wonder! They go in large parties with
mules and horses; they make a great noise; they are dressed
in outlandish, unnatural colors; every animal shuns them.
Even the frightened pines would run away if they could.
But Nature-lovers, devout, silent, open-eyed, looking and
listening with love, find no lack of inhabitants in these
mountain mansions, and they come to them gladly. Not to
mention the large animals or the small insect people, every
waterfall has its ouzel and every tree its squirrel or tamias
or bird: tiny nuthatch threading the furrows of the bark,
cheerily whispering to itself as it deftly pries off loose scales

47

and examines the curled edges of lichens; or Clarke crow or jay examining the cones; or some singer—oriole, tanager, warbler—resting, feeding, attending to domestic affairs. Hawks and eagles sail overhead, grouse walk in happy flocks below, and song sparrows sing in every bed of chaparral. There is no crowding, to be sure. Unlike the low Eastern trees, those of the Sierra in the main forest belt average nearly two hundred feet in height, and of course many birds are required to make much show in them, and many voices to fill them. Nevertheless, the whole range, from foothills to snowy summits, is shaken into song every summer; and though low and thin in winter, the music never ceases.

The sage cock (*Centrocercus urophasianus*) is the largest of the Sierra game-birds and the king of American grouse. It is an admirably strong, hardy, handsome, independent bird, able with comfort to bid defiance to heat, cold, drought, hunger, and all sorts of storms, living on whatever seeds or insects chance to come in its way, or simply on the leaves of sage-brush, everywhere abundant on its desert range. In winter, when the temperature is oftentimes below zero, and heavy snowstorms are blowing, he sits beneath a sage-bush and allows himself to be covered, poking his head now and then through the snow to feed on the leaves of his shelter. Not even the Arctic ptarmigan is hardier in braving frost and snow and wintry darkness. When in full plumage he is a beautiful bird, with a long, firm, sharp-pointed tail, which in walking is slightly raised and swings sidewise back and forth with each step. The male is handsomely marked with black and white on the neck, back, and wings, weighs five or six pounds, and measures about thirty inches in length. The female is clad mostly in plain brown, and is not so large. They occasionally wander from the sage plains into the open nut-pine and juniper woods, but never enter the main coniferous forest. It is only in the broad, dry, half-desert sage plains that they are quite at home, where the weather is blazing hot in summer, cold in winter. If any one passes through a flock, all squat on the gray ground and hold their heads low, hoping to escape observation; but when approached within a rod or so, they rise with a magnificent burst of wing-beats, looking about as big as turkeys and making a noise like a whirlwind.

On the 28th of June, at the head of Owen's Valley, I caught one of the young that was then just able to fly. It was seven inches long, of a uniform gray color, blunt-billed, and when captured cried lustily in a shrill piping voice, clear in tone as a boy's small willow whistle. I have seen flocks of from ten to thirty or forty on the east margin of the Park, where the Mono Desert meets the gray foothills of the Sierra; but since cattle have been pastured there they are becoming rarer every year.

Another magnificent bird, the blue or dusky grouse, next in size to the sage cock, is found all through the main forest belt, though not in great numbers. They like best the heaviest silver-fir woods near garden and meadow openings, where there is but little underbrush to cover the approach of enemies. When a flock of these brave birds,

49

✱ Birds ✱

sauntering and feeding on the sunny, flowery levels of some hidden meadow or Yosemite valley far back in the heart of the mountains, see a man for the first time in their lives, they rise with hurried notes of surprise and excitement and alight on the lowest branches of the trees, wondering what the wanderer may be, and showing great eagerness to get a good view of the strange vertical animal. Knowing nothing of guns, they allow you to approach within a half dozen paces, then quietly hop a few branches higher or fly to the next tree without a thought of concealment, so that you may observe them as long as you like, near enough to see the fine shading of their plumage, the feathers on their toes, and the innocent wonderment in their beautiful wild eyes. But in the neighborhood of roads and trails they soon become shy, and when disturbed fly into the highest, leafiest trees, and suddenly become invisible, so well do they know how to hide and keep still and make use of their protective coloring. Nor can they be easily dislodged ere they are ready to go. In vain the hunter goes round and round some tall pine or fir into which he has perhaps seen a dozen enter, gazing up through the branches, straining his eyes while his gun is held ready; not a feather can he see unless his eyes have been sharpened by long experience and knowledge of the blue grouse's habits. Then, perhaps, when he is thinking that the tree must be hollow and that the birds have all gone inside, they burst forth with a startling whir of wing-beats, and after gaining full speed go skating swiftly away through the forest arches in a long, silent, wavering slide, with wings held steady.

* Among the Birds of the Yosemite *

During the summer they are most of the time on the
ground, feeding on insects, seeds, berries, etc., around the
margins of open spots and rocky moraines, playing and
sauntering, taking sun baths and sand baths, and drinking
at little pools and rills during the heat of the day. In winter
they live mostly in the trees, depending on buds for food,
sheltering beneath dense overlapping branches at night
and during storms on the leeside of the trunk, sunning
themselves on the southside limbs in fine weather, and
sometimes diving into the mealy snow to flutter and wallow, apparently for exercise and fun.

I have seen young broods running beneath the firs in
June at a height of eight thousand feet above the sea. On
the approach of danger, the mother with a peculiar cry
warns the helpless midgets to scatter and hide beneath
leaves and twigs, and even in plain open places it is almost
impossible to discover them. In the meantime the mother
feigns lameness, throws herself at your feet, kicks and
gasps and flutters, to draw your attention from the chicks.
The young are generally able to fly about the middle of
July; but even after they can fly well they are usually advised to run and hide and lie still, no matter how closely
approached, while the mother goes on with her loving,
lying acting, apparently as desperately concerned for their
safety as when they were featherless infants. Sometimes,
however, after carefully studying the circumstances, she
tells them to take wing; and up and away in a blurry birr
and whir they scatter to all points of the compass, as if
blown up with gunpowder, dropping cunningly out of

sight three or four hundred yards off, and keeping quiet
until called, after the danger is supposed to be past. If you
walk on a little way without manifesting any inclination to
hunt them, you may sit down at the foot of a tree near
enough to see and hear the happy reunion. One touch of
nature makes the whole world kin; and it is truly wonderful
how love-telling the small voices of these birds are, and
how far they reach through the woods into one another's
hearts and into ours. The tones are so perfectly human and
so full of anxious affection, few mountaineers can fail to be
touched by them.

They are cared for until full grown. On the 20th of
August, as I was passing along the margin of a garden spot
on the head-waters of the San Joaquin, a grouse rose from
the ruins of an old juniper that had been uprooted and
brought down by an avalanche from a cliff overhead. She
threw herself at my feet, limped and fluttered and gasped,
showing, as I thought, that she had a nest and was raising a
second brood. Looking for the eggs, I was surprised to see
a strong-winged flock nearly as large as the mother fly up
around me.

Instead of seeking a warmer climate when the winter
storms set in, these hardy birds stay all the year in the high
Sierra forests, and I have never known them to suffer in
any sort of weather. Able to live on the buds of pine,
spruce, and fir, they are forever independent in the matter
of food supply, which gives so many of us trouble, dragging us here and there away from our best work. How
gladly I would live on pine buds, however pitchy, for the

sake of this grand independence! With all his superior resources, man makes more distracting difficulty concerning food than any other of the family.

The mountain quail, or plumed partridge (*Oreortyx pictus plumiferus*), is common in all the upper portions of the Park, though nowhere in numbers. He ranges considerably higher than the grouse in summer, but is unable to endure the heavy storms of winter. When his food is buried, he descends the range to the brushy foothills, at a height of from two thousand to three thousand feet above the sea; but like every true mountaineer, he is quick to follow the spring back into the highest mountains. I think he is the very handsomest and most interesting of all the American partridges, larger and handsomer than the famous Bob White, or even the fine California valley quail, or the Massena partridge of Arizona and Mexico. That he is not so regarded, is because as a lonely mountaineer he is not half known.

His plumage is delicately shaded, brown above, white and rich chestnut below and on the sides, with many dainty markings of black and white and gray here and there, while his beautiful head plume, three or four inches long, nearly straight, composed of two feathers closely folded so as to appear as one, is worn jauntily slanted backward like a single feather in a boy's cap, giving him a very marked appearance. They wander over the lonely mountains in family flocks of from six to fifteen, beneath ceanothus, manzanita, and wild cherry thickets, and over dry sandy flats, glacier meadows, rocky ridges, and beds of bryanthus around glacier lakes, especially in autumn, when the berries of the upper gardens are ripe, uttering low clucking notes to enable them to keep together. When they are so suddenly disturbed that they are afraid they cannot escape the danger by running into thickets, they rise with a fine hearty whir and scatter in the brush over an area of half a square mile or so, a few of them diving into leafy trees. But as soon as the danger is past, the parents with a clear piping note call them together again. By the end of July the young are two thirds grown and fly well, though only dire necessity can compel them to try their wings. In gait, gestures, habits, and general behavior they are like domestic chickens, but infinitely finer, searching for insects and seeds, looking to this side and that, scratching among fallen leaves, jumping up to pull down grass heads, and clucking and muttering in low tones.

Once when I was seated at the foot of a tree on the headwaters of the Merced, sketching, I heard a flock up the valley behind me, and by their voices gradually sounding nearer I knew that they were feeding toward me. I kept still, hoping to see them. Soon one came within three or four feet of me, without noticing me any more than if I were a stump or a bulging part of the trunk against which I was leaning, my clothing being brown, nearly like the bark. Presently along came another and another, and it was delightful to get so near a view of these handsome chickens perfectly undisturbed, observe their manners, and hear their low peaceful notes. At last one of them caught my eye, gazed in silent wonder for a moment, then uttered a peculiar cry, which was followed by a lot of hurried muttered notes that sounded like speech. The others, of course, saw me as soon as the alarm was sounded, and joined the wonder talk, gazing and chattering, astonished but not frightened. Then all with one accord ran back with the news to the rest of the flock. "What is it? what is it? Oh, you never saw the like," they seemed to be saying. "Not a deer, or a wolf, or a bear; come see, come see." "Where? where?" "Down there by that tree." Then they approached cautiously, past the tree, stretching their necks, and looking up in turn as if knowing from the story told them just where I was. For fifteen or twenty minutes they kept coming and going, venturing within a few feet of me, and discussing the wonder in charming chatter. Their curiosity at last satisfied, they began to scatter and feed again, going back in the direction they had come from; while I, loath to part with them, followed noiselessly, crawling beneath the bushes, keeping them in sight for an hour or two, learning their habits, and finding out what seeds and berries they liked best.

The valley quail is not a mountaineer, and seldom enters the Park except at a few of the lowest places on the western boundary. It belongs to the brushy foothills and plains, orchards and wheatfields, and is a hundred times more numerous than the mountain quail. It is a beautiful bird, about the size of the Bob White, and has a handsome crest of four or five feathers an inch long, recurved, standing nearly erect at times or drooping forward. The loud calls of these quails in the spring—Pe-check-ah, Pe-check-a, Hoy, Hoy—are heard far and near over all the lowlands.

* Birds *

They have vastly increased in numbers since the settlement
of the country, notwithstanding the immense numbers
killed every season by boys and pot-hunters as well as the
regular leggined sportsmen from the towns; for man's destructive action is more than counterbalanced by increased
supply of food from cultivation, and by the destruction of
their enemies—coyotes, skunks, foxes, hawks, owls,
etc.—which not only kill the old birds, but plunder their
nests. Where coyotes and skunks abound, scarce one pair
in a hundred is successful in raising a brood. So well aware
are these birds of the protection afforded by man, even now
that the number of their wild enemies has been greatly
diminished, that they prefer to nest near houses, notwithstanding they are so shy. Four or five pairs rear their young
around our cottage every spring. One year a pair nested in
a straw pile within four or five feet of the stable door, and
did not leave the eggs when the men led the horses back and
forth within a foot or two. For many seasons a pair nested
in a tuft of pampas grass in the garden; another pair in an
ivy vine on the cottage roof, and when the young were
hatched, it was interesting to see the parents getting the
fluffy dots down. They were greatly excited, and their anxious calls and directions to their many babes attracted our
attention. They had no great difficulty in persuading the
young birds to pitch themselves from the main roof to the
porch roof among the ivy, but to get them safely down
from the latter to the ground, a distance of ten feet, was
most distressing. It seemed impossible the frail soft things
could avoid being killed. The anxious parents led them to

a point above a spiræa bush, that reached nearly to the eaves, which they seemed to know would break the fall. Anyhow they led their chicks to this point, and with infinite coaxing and encouragement got them to tumble themselves off. Down they rolled and sifted through the soft leaves and panicles to the pavement, and, strange to say, all got away unhurt except one that lay as if dead for a few minutes. When it revived, the joyful parents, with their brood fairly launched on the journey of life, proudly led them down the cottage hill, through the garden, and along an osage orange hedge into the cherry orchard. These charming birds even enter towns and villages, where the gardens are of good size and guns are forbidden, sometimes going several miles to feed, and returning every evening to their roosts in ivy or brushy trees and shrubs.

Geese occasionally visit the Park, but never stay long. Sometimes on their way across the range, a flock wanders into Hetch-Hetchy or Yosemite to rest or get something to eat, and if shot at, are often sorely bewildered in seeking a way out. I have seen them rise from the meadow or river, wheel round in a spiral until a height of four or five hundred feet was reached, then form ranks and try to fly over the wall. But Yosemite magnitudes seem to be as deceptive to geese as to men, for they would suddenly find themselves against the cliffs not a fourth of the way to the top. Then turning in confusion, and screaming at the strange heights, they would try the opposite side, and so on until exhausted they were compelled to rest, and only after discovering the river cañon could they make their escape. Large, harrow-shaped flocks may often be seen crossing the range in the spring, at a height of at least fourteen thousand feet. Think of the strength of wing required to sustain so heavy a bird in air so thin. At this elevation it is but little over half as dense as at the sea level. Yet they hold bravely on in beautifully dressed ranks, and have breath enough to spare for loud honking. After the crest of the Sierra is passed it is only a smooth slide down the sky to the waters of Mono, where they may rest as long as they like.

Ducks of five or six species, among which are the mallard and wood duck, go far up into the heart of the mountains in the spring, and of course come down in the fall with the families they have reared. A few, as if loath to leave the mountains, pass the winter in the lower valleys of the Park at a height of three thousand to four thousand feet, where the main streams are never wholly frozen over, and snow never falls to a great depth or lies long. In summer they are found up to a height of eleven thousand feet on all the lakes and branches of the rivers except the smallest, and those beside the glaciers incumbered with drifting ice and snow. I found mallards and wood ducks at Lake Tenaya, June 1, before the ice-covering was half melted, and a flock of young ones in Bloody Cañon Lake, June 20. They are usually met in pairs, never in large flocks. No place is too wild or rocky or solitary for these brave swimmers, no stream too rapid. In the roaring, resounding cañon torrents, they seem as much at home as in the tranquil reaches and lakes of the broad glacial valleys. Abandoning themselves to the wild play of the waters, they go drifting confidingly through blinding, thrashing spray, dancing on boulder-dashed waves, tossing in beautiful security on rougher water than is usually encountered by sea birds when storms are blowing.

A mother duck with her family of ten little ones, waltzing round and round in a pot-hole ornamented with foam bells, huge rocks leaning over them, cascades above and below and beside them, made one of the most interesting bird pictures I ever saw.

I have never found the great northern diver in the Park lakes. Most of them are inaccessible to him. He might plump down into them, but would hardly be able to get out of them, since, with his small wings and heavy body, a wide expanse of elbow room is required in rising. Now and then one may be seen in the lower Sierra lakes to the northward about Lassens Butte and Shasta, at a height of four thousand to five thousand feet, making the loneliest places lonelier with the wildest of wild cries.

Plovers are found along the sandy shores of nearly all the mountain lakes, tripping daintily on the water's edge, picking up insects; and it is interesting to learn how few of these familiar birds are required to make a solitude cheerful.

Sandhill cranes are sometimes found in comparatively small marshes, mere dots in the mighty forest. In such spots, at an elevation of from six thousand to eight thousand feet above the sea, they are occasionally met in pairs as early as the end of May, while the snow is still deep in the surrounding fir and sugar-pine woods. And on sunny days in autumn, large flocks may be seen sailing at a great height above the forests, shaking the crisp air into rolling waves with their hearty koor-r-r, koor-r-r, uck-uck, soaring in circles for hours together on their majestic wings, seeming to float without effort like clouds, eying the wrinkled landscape outspread like a map mottled with lakes and glaciers and meadows and streaked with shadowy cañons and streams, and surveying every frog marsh and sandy flat within a hundred miles.

Eagles and hawks are oftentimes seen above the ridges and domes. The greatest height at which I have observed them was about twelve thousand feet, over the summits of Mount Hoffman, in the middle region of the Park. A few pairs had their nests on the cliffs of this mountain, and could be seen every day in summer, hunting marmots, mountain beavers, pikas, etc. A pair of golden eagles have made their home in Yosemite ever since I went there thirty years ago. Their nest is on the Nevada Fall Cliff, opposite the Liberty Cap. Their screams are rather pleasant to hear in the vast gulfs between the granite cliffs, and they help the owls in keeping the echoes busy.

But of all the birds of the high Sierra, the strangest, noisiest, and most notable is the Clarke crow (*Nucifraga columbiana*). He is a foot long and nearly two feet in extent of wing, ashy gray in general color, with black wings, white tail, and a strong, sharp bill, with which he digs into the pine cones for the seeds on which he mainly subsists. He is quick, boisterous, jerky, and irregular in his movements and speech, and makes a tremendously loud and showy advertisement of himself,—swooping and diving in deep curves across gorges and valleys from ridge to ridge, alighting on dead spars, looking warily about him, and leaving his dry, springy perches trembling from the vigor of his kick as he launches himself for a new flight, screaming from time to time loud enough to be heard more than a mile in still weather. He dwells far back on the high stormbeaten margin of the forest, where the mountain pine, juniper, and hemlock grow wide apart on glacier pavements and domes and rough crumbling ridges, and the dwarf pine makes a low crinkled growth along the flanks of the Summit peaks. In so open a region, of course, he is well seen. Everybody notices him, and nobody at first knows what to make of him. One guesses he must be a woodpecker; another a crow or some sort of jay, another a magpie. He seems to be a pretty thoroughly mixed and fermented compound of all these birds, has all their strength, cunning, shyness, thievishness, and wary, suspicious curiosity combined and condensed. He flies like a woodpecker, hammers dead limbs for insects, digs big holes in pine cones to get at the seeds, cracks nuts held between his toes, cries like a crow or Steller jay,—but in a far louder, harsher, and more forbidding tone of voice,—and besides his crow caws and screams, has a great variety of small chatter talk, mostly uttered in a fault-finding tone. Like the magpie, he steals articles that can be of no use to him. Once when I made my camp in a grove at Cathedral Lake, I chanced to leave a cake of soap on the shore where I had been washing, and a few minutes afterward I saw my

* Birds *

soap flying past me through the grove, pushed by a Clarke crow.

In winter, when the snow is deep, the cones of the mountain pines are empty, and the juniper, hemlock, and dwarf pine orchard buried, he comes down to glean seeds in the yellow pine forests, startling the grouse with his loud screams. But even in winter, in calm weather, he stays in his high mountain home, defying the bitter frost. Once I lay snowbound through a three days' storm at the timberline on Mount Shasta; and while the roaring snow-laden blast swept by, one of these brave birds came to my camp, and began hammering at the cones on the topmost branches of half-buried pines, without showing the slightest distress. I have seen Clarke crows feeding their young as early as June 19, at a height of more than ten thousand feet, when nearly the whole landscape was snow-covered.

They are excessively shy, and keep away from the traveler as long as they think they are observed; but when one goes on without seeming to notice them, or sits down and keeps still, their curiosity speedily gets the better of their caution, and they come flying from tree to tree, nearer and nearer, and watch every motion. Few, I am afraid, will ever learn to like this bird, he is so suspicious and self-reliant, and his voice is so harsh that to most ears the scream of the eagle will seem melodious compared with it. Yet the mountaineer who has battled and suffered and struggled must admire his strength and endurance,—the way he faces the mountain weather, cleaves the icy blasts, cares for his young, and digs a living from the stern wilderness.

* Among the Birds of the Yosemite *

Higher yet than Nucifraga dwells the little dun-headed sparrow (*Leucosticte tephrocotis*). From early spring to late autumn he is to be found only on the snowy, icy peaks at the head of the glacier cirques and cañons. His feeding grounds in spring are the snow sheets between the peaks, and in midsummer and autumn the glaciers. Many bold insects go mountaineering almost as soon as they are born, ascending the highest summits on the mild breezes that blow in from the sea every day during steady weather; but comparatively few of these adventurers find their way down or see a flower bed again. Getting tired and chilly, they alight on the snow fields and glaciers, attracted perhaps by the glare, take cold, and die. There they lie as if on a white cloth purposely outspread for them, and the dun sparrows find them a rich and varied repast requiring no pursuit,—bees and butterflies on ice, and many spicy beetles, a perpetual feast, on tables big for guests so small, and in vast banqueting halls ventilated by cool breezes that ruffle the feathers of the fairy brownies. Happy fellows, no rivals come to dispute possession with them. No other birds, not even hawks, as far as I have noticed, live so high. They see people so seldom, they flutter around the explorer with the liveliest curiosity, and come down a little way, sometimes nearly a mile, to meet him and conduct him into their icy homes.

When I was exploring the Merced group, climbing up the grand cañon between the Merced and Red mountains into the fountain amphitheatre of an ancient glacier, just as I was approaching the small active glacier that leans back

63

* Birds *

in the shadow of Merced Mountain, a flock of twenty or thirty of these little birds, the first I had seen, came down the cañon to meet me, flying low, straight toward me as if they meant to fly in my face. Instead of attacking me or passing by, they circled round my head, chirping and fluttering for a minute or two, then turned and escorted me up the cañon, alighting on the nearest rocks on either hand, and flying ahead a few yards at a time to keep even with me.

I have not discovered their winter quarters. Probably they are in the desert ranges to the eastward, for I never saw any of them in Yosemite, the winter refuge of so many of the mountain birds.

Humming-birds are among the best and most conspicuous of the mountaineers, flashing their ruby throats in countless wild gardens far up the higher slopes, where they would be least expected. All one has to do to enjoy the company of these mountain-loving midgets is to display a showy blanket or handkerchief.

The arctic bluebird is another delightful mountaineer, singing a wild, cheery song and "carrying the sky on his back" over all the gray ridges and domes of the subalpine region.

A fine, hearty, good-natured lot of woodpeckers dwell in the Park, and keep it lively all the year round. Among the most notable of these are the magnificent log cock (*Ceophlœus pileatus*), the prince of Sierra woodpeckers, and only second in rank, as far as I know, of all the woodpeckers of the world; the Lewis woodpecker, large, black, glossy, that flaps and flies like a crow, does but little hammering,

64

* Among the Birds of the Yosemite *

and feeds in great part on wild cherries and berries; and the carpenter, who stores up great quantities of acorns in the bark of trees for winter use. The last-named species is a beautiful bird, and far more common than the others. In the woods of the West he represents the Eastern red-head. Bright, cheerful, industrious, not in the least shy, the carpenters give delightful animation to the open Sierra forests at a height of from three thousand to fifty-five hundred feet, especially in autumn, when the acorns are ripe. Then no squirrel works harder at his pine-nut harvest than these woodpeckers at their acorn harvest, drilling holes in the thick, corky bark of the yellow pine and incense cedar, in which to store the crop for winter use,—a hole for each acorn, so nicely adjusted as to size that when the acorn, point foremost, is driven in, it fits so well that it cannot be drawn out without digging around it. Each acorn is thus carefully stored in a dry bin, perfectly protected from the weather,—a most laborious method of stowing away a crop, a granary for each kernel. Yet the birds seem never to weary at the work, but go on so diligently that they seem determined to save every acorn in the grove. They are never seen eating acorns at the time they are storing them, and it is commonly believed that they never eat them or intend to eat them, but that the wise birds store them and protect them from the depredations of squirrels and jays, solely for the sake of the worms they are supposed to contain. And because these worms are too small for use at the time the acorns drop, they are shut up like lean calves and steers, each in a separate stall with abundance of food, to grow big and fat by the time they will be most wanted, that is, in winter, when insects are scarce and stall-fed worms most valuable. So these woodpeckers are supposed to be a sort of cattle-raisers, each with a drove of thousands, rivaling the ants that raise grain and keep herds of plant lice for milk cows. Needless to say the story is not true, though some naturalists, even, believe it. When Emerson was in the Park, having heard the worm story and seen the great pines plugged full of acorns, he asked (just to pump me, I suppose), "Why do the woodpeckers take the trouble to put acorns into the bark of the trees?" "For the same reason," I replied, "that bees store honey and squirrels nuts." "But they tell me, Mr. Muir, that woodpeckers don't eat acorns." "Yes, they do," I said, "I have seen them eating them. During snowstorms they seem to eat little besides acorns. I have repeatedly interrupted them at their meals, and seen the perfectly sound, half-eaten acorns. They eat them in the shell as some people eat eggs." "But what about the worms?" "I suppose," I said, "that when they come to a wormy one they eat both worm and acorn. Anyhow, they eat the sound ones when they can't find anything they like better, and from the time they store them until they are used they guard them, and woe to the squirrel or jay caught stealing." Indians, in times of scarcity, frequently resort to these stores and chop them out with hatchets; a bushel or more may be gathered from a single cedar or pine.

The common robin, with all his familiar notes and gestures, is found nearly everywhere throughout the Park,—in shady dells beneath dogwoods and maples, along the flowery banks of the streams, tripping daintily about the margins of meadows in the fir and pine woods, and far beyond on the shores of glacier lakes and the slopes of the peaks. How admirable the constitution and temper of this cheery, graceful bird, keeping glad health over so vast and varied a range! In all America he is at home, flying from plains to mountains, up and down, north and south, away and back, with the seasons and supply of food. Oftentimes in the High Sierra, as you wander through the solemn woods, awe-stricken and silent, you will hear the reassuring voice of this fellow wanderer ringing out sweet and clear as if saying, "Fear not, fear not. Only love is here." In the severest solitudes he seems as happy as in gardens and apple orchards.

The robins enter the Park as soon as the snow melts, and go on up the mountains, gradually higher, with the opening flowers, until the topmost glacier meadows are reached in June and July. After the short summer is done, they descend like most other summer visitors in concord with the weather, keeping out of the first heavy snows as much as possible, while lingering among the frost-nipped wild cherries on the slopes just below the glacier meadows. Thence they go to the lower slopes of the forest region, compelled to make haste at times by heavy all-day storms, picking up seeds or benumbed insects by the way; and at last all, save a few that winter in Yosemite valleys, arrive in the vineyards and orchards and stubble-fields of the lowlands in November, picking up fallen fruit and grain, and awakening old-time memories among the white-headed pioneers, who cannot fail to recognize the influence of so homelike a bird. They are then in flocks of hundreds, and make their way into the gardens of towns as well as into the parks and fields and orchards about the bay of San Francisco, where many of the wanderers are shot for sport and the morsel of meat on their breasts. Man then seems a beast of prey. Not even genuine piety can make the robin-killer quite respectable. Saturday is the great slaughter day in the bay region. Then the city pot-hunters, with a rag-tag of boys, go forth to kill, kept in countenance by a sprinkling of regular sportsmen arrayed in self-conscious majesty and leggins, leading dogs and carrying hammerless, breech-loading guns of famous makers. Over the fine landscapes the killing goes forward with shameful enthusiasm. After escaping countless dangers, thousands fall, big bagfuls are gathered, many are left wounded to die slowly, no Red Cross Society to help them. Next day, Sunday, the blood and leggins vanish from the most devout of the bird-butchers, who go to church, carrying gold-headed canes instead of guns. After hymns, prayers, and sermon they go home to feast, to put God's song birds to use, put them in their dinners instead of in their hearts, eat them, and suck the pitiful little drumsticks. It is only race living on race, to be sure, but Christians singing Divine Love need not be driven to such straits while wheat and apples grow and the shops are full of dead cattle. Song birds for food! Compared with this, making kindlings of pianos and violins would be pious economy.

The larks come in large flocks from the hills and moun-

Muir with "Stickeen" under tree, 1905. Bancroft Library,
University of California at Berkeley.

"Wild Sheep," W. M. Cary, artist. From *Picturesque California*.

"A Herd of Elk, Pitt River Canyon," Thomas Hill, artist.
From *Picturesque California*.

"The Illilouette Falls,"
Thomas Hill, artist.
From *Picturesque
California*.

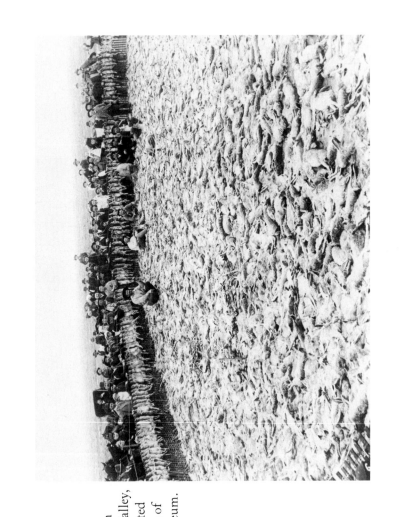

Rabbit hunt in
San Joaquin Valley,
1892. Reprinted
by permission of
Haggin Museum.

"After a Good Day's Sport," F. O. C. Darley, artist. From *Picturesque California*.

"Encounter with a Grizzly Bear," Thomas Hill, artist. From *Picturesque California*.

Alligator eating man in Florida, 1868. John Muir Papers,
Holt-Atherton Center for Western Studies, University of the
Pacific. Copyright 1984 Muir-Hanna Trust.

Sheep grazing in Yosemite, 1900. Yosemite Research Library.

Animals cruelly brought to slaughter in Cuba, 1868. John Muir Papers, Holt-Atherton Center for Western Studies, University of the Pacific. Copyright 1984 Muir-Hanna Trust.

tains in the fall, and are slaughtered as ruthlessly as the robins. Fortunately, most of our song birds keep back in leafy hidings, and are comparatively inaccessible.

The water ouzel, in his rocky home amid foaming waters, seldom sees a gun, and of all the singers I like him the best. He is a plainly dressed little bird, about the size of a robin, with short, crisp, but rather broad wings, and a tail of moderate length, slanted up, giving him, with his nodding, bobbing manners, a wrennish look. He is usually seen fluttering about in the spray of falls and the rapid cascading portions of the main branches of the rivers. These are his favorite haunts; but he is often seen also on comparatively level reaches and occasionally on the shores of mountain lakes, especially at the beginning of winter, when heavy snowfalls have blurred the streams with sludge. Though not a water-bird in structure, he gets his living in the water, and is never seen away from the immediate margin of streams. He dives fearlessly into rough, boiling eddies and rapids to feed at the bottom, flying under water seemingly as easily as in the air. Sometimes he wades in shallow places, thrusting his head under from time to time in a nodding, frisky way that is sure to attract attention. His flight is a solid whir of wing-beats like that of a partridge, and in going from place to place along his favorite string of rapids he follows the windings of the stream, and usually alights on some rock or snag on the bank or out in the current, or rarely on the dry limb of an overhanging tree, perching like a tree bird when it suits his convenience. He has the oddest, neatest manners imaginable, and all his gestures as he flits about in the wild, dashing waters bespeak the utmost cheerfulness and confidence. He sings both winter and summer, in all sorts of weather,—a sweet, fluty melody, rather low, and much less keen and accentuated than from the brisk vigor of his movements one would be led to expect.

How romantic and beautiful is the life of this brave little singer on the wild mountain streams, building his round bossy nest of moss by the side of a rapid or fall, where it is sprinkled and kept fresh and green by the spray! No wonder he sings well, since all the air about him is music; every breath he draws is part of a song, and he gets his first music lessons before he is born; for the eggs vibrate in time with the tones of the waterfalls. Bird and stream are inseparable, songful and wild, gentle and strong,—the bird ever in danger in the midst of the stream's mad whirlpools, yet seemingly immortal. And so I might go on, writing words, words, words; but to what purpose? Go see him and love him, and through him as through a window look into Nature's warm heart.

The Passenger
Pigeon

IT WAS A GREAT MEMORABLE DAY WHEN
the first flock of passenger pigeons came to our farm, calling to mind the story we had read about them when we
were at school in Scotland. Of all God's feathered people
that sailed the Wisconsin sky, no other bird seemed to us so
wonderful. The beautiful wanderers flew like the winds in
flocks of millions from climate to climate in accord with
the weather, finding their food—acorns, beechnuts, pine-
nuts, cranberries, strawberries, huckleberries, juniper
berries, hackberries, buckwheat, rice, wheat, oats, corn—
in fields and forests thousands of miles apart. I have seen
flocks streaming south in the fall so large that they were
flowing over from horizon to horizon in an almost continuous stream all day long, at the rate of forty or fifty miles
an hour, like a mighty river in the sky, widening, contract-

ing, descending like falls and cataracts, and rising suddenly here and there in huge ragged masses like high-plashing
spray. How wonderful the distances they flew in a day—in
a year—in a lifetime! They arrived in Wisconsin in the
spring just after the sun had cleared away the snow, and
alighted in the woods to feed on the fallen acorns that they
had missed the previous autumn. A comparatively small
flock swept thousands of acres perfectly clean of acorns in a
few minutes, by moving straight ahead with a broad front.
All got their share, for the rear constantly became the van
by flying over the flock and alighting in front, the entire
flock constantly changing from rear to front, revolving
something like a wheel with a low buzzing wing roar that
could be heard a long way off. In summer they feasted on
wheat and oats and were easily approached as they rested on
the trees along the sides of the field after a good full meal,
displaying beautiful iridescent colors as they moved their
necks backward and forward when we went very near
them. Every shotgun was aimed at them and everybody
feasted on pigeon pies, and not a few of the settlers feasted
also on the beauty of the wonderful birds. The breast of the
male is a fine rosy red, the lower part of the neck behind
and along the sides changing from the red of the breast to
gold, emerald green and rich crimson. The general color
of the upper parts is grayish blue, the under parts white.
The extreme length of the bird is about seventeen inches;
the finely modeled slender tail about eight inches, and extent of wings twenty-four inches. The females are scarcely

less beautiful. "Oh, what bonnie, bonnie birds!" we exclaimed over the first that fell into our hands. "Oh, what colors! Look at their breasts, bonnie as roses, and at their necks aglow wi' every color juist like the wonderfu' wood ducks. Oh, the bonnie, bonnie creatures, they beat a'! Where did they a' come fra, and where are they a' gan? It's awfu' like a sin to kill them!" To this some smug, practical old sinner would remark: "Aye, it's a peety, as ye say, to kill the bonnie things, but they were made to be killed, and sent for us to eat as the quails were sent to God's chosen people, the Israelites, when they were starving in the desert ayont the Red Sea. And I must confess that meat was never put up in neater, handsomer-painted packages."

In the New England and Canada woods beechnuts were their best and most abundant food, farther north, cranberries and huckleberries. After everything was cleaned up in the north and winter was coming on, they went south for rice, corn, acorns, haws, wild grapes, crab-apples, sparkle-berries, etc. They seemed to require more than half of the continent for feeding-grounds, moving from one table to another, field to field, forest to forest, finding something ripe and wholesome all the year round. In going south in the fine Indian-summer weather they flew high and followed one another, though the head of the flock might be hundreds of miles in advance. But against head winds they took advantage of the inequalities of the ground, flying comparatively low. All followed the leader's ups and downs over hill and dale though far out of sight, never hesitating at any turn of the way, vertical or horizontal that the leaders had taken, though the largest flocks stretched across several States, and belts of different kinds of weather.

There were no roosting- or breeding-places near our farm, and I never saw any of them until long after the great flocks were exterminated. I therefore quote, from Audubon's and Pokagon's vivid descriptions.

"Toward evening," Audubon says, "they depart for the roosting-place, which may be hundreds of miles distant. One on the banks of Green River, Kentucky, was over three miles wide and forty long."

"My first view of it," says the great naturalist, "was about a fortnight after it had been chosen by the birds, and I arrived there nearly two hours before sunset. Few pigeons were then to be seen, but a great many persons with horses and wagons and armed with guns, long poles, sulphur pots, pine pitch torches, etc., had already established encampments on the borders. Two farmers had driven upwards of three hundred hogs a distance of more than a hundred miles to be fattened on slaughtered pigeons. Here and there the people employed in plucking and salting what had already been secured were sitting in the midst of piles of birds. Dung several inches thick covered the ground. Many trees two feet in diameter were broken off at no great distance from the ground, and the branches of many of the tallest and largest had given way, as if the forest had been swept by a tornado.

"Not a pigeon had arrived at sundown. Suddenly a general cry arose—'Here they come!' The noise they made, though still distant, reminded me of a hard gale at sea passing through the rigging of a close-reefed ship. Thousands were soon knocked down by the pole-men. The birds continued to pour in. The fires were lighted and a magnificent as well as terrifying sight presented itself. The pigeons pouring in alighted everywhere, one above another, until solid masses were formed on the branches all around. Here and there the perches gave way with a crash, and falling destroyed hundreds beneath, forcing down the dense groups with which every stick was loaded; a scene of uproar and conflict. I found it useless to speak or even to shout to those persons nearest me. Even the reports of the guns were seldom heard, and I was made aware of the firing only by seeing the shooters reloading. None dared venture within the line of devastation. The hogs had been penned up in due time, the picking up of the dead and wounded being left for the next morning's employment. The pigeons were constantly coming in and it was after midnight before I perceived a decrease in the number of those that arrived. The uproar continued all night, and, anxious to know how far the sound reached I sent off a man who, returning two hours after, informed me that he had heard it distinctly three miles distant.

"Toward daylight the noise in some measure subsided; long before objects were distinguishable the pigeons began to move off in a direction quite different from that in which they had arrived the evening before, and at sunrise all that were able to fly had disappeared. The howling of the wolves now reached our ears, and the foxes, lynxes, cougars, bears, coons, opossums, and polecats were seen sneaking off, while eagles and hawks of different species, accompanied by a crowd of vultures, came to supplant them and enjoy a share of the spoil.

"Then the authors of all this devastation began their entry amongst the dead, the dying and mangled. The pigeons were picked up and piled in heaps until each had as many as they could possibly dispose of, when the hogs were let loose to feed on the remainder.

"The breeding-places are selected with reference to abundance of food, and countless myriads resort to them. At this period the note of the pigeon is *coo coo coo*, like that of the domestic species but much shorter. They caress by billing, and during incubation the male supplies the female with food. As the young grow, the tyrant of creation appears to disturb the peaceful scene, armed with axes to chop down the squab-laden trees, and the abomination of desolation and destruction produced far surpasses even that of the roosting places."

Pokagon, an educated Indian writer, says: "I saw one nesting-place in Wisconsin one hundred miles long and from three to ten miles wide. Every tree, some of them quite low and scrubby, had from one to fifty nests on each. Some of the nests overflow from the oaks to the hemlock and pine woods. When the pigeon hunters attack the breeding-places they sometimes cut the timber from thou-

* The Passenger Pigeon *

sands of acres. Millions are caught in nets with salt or grain for bait, and schooners, sometimes loaded down with the birds, are taken to New York, where they are sold for a cent apiece."

CHAPTER THREE

*

DOMESTIC ANIMALS

Rarely did John Muir write about domestic animals. Most of his descriptions of tame creatures appeared in The Story of My Boyhood and Youth, *written toward the end of his life. Even these were limited to pets and beasts of burden; Muir had nothing but disdain for cattle and sheep.*

His earlier works contained fewer references to domestic animals. The dog Carlo—Muir's companion during his sheepherding days—received little attention in My First Summer in the Sierra; *similarly, it was thirty years before his adventure with Stickeen—which occurred in 1879—was finally written and published. Certainly he was far more interested in wild animals.*

Yet Muir developed an increasing affinity for tame creatures. Late in life, he kept a variety of pets, becoming particularly fond of a cat to whom he threw scraps from the dinner table.

While he published little on domestic animals, Muir's affection for these creatures was given eloquent voice in his most famous work, the story of Stickeen. This dog was, in fact, "the herald of a new gospel"—that of the link between man and other animals. "I have known many dogs," Muir wrote of his companion, "but to none do I owe so much as to Stickeen. At first the least promising and least known of my dog-friends, he suddenly became the best known of them all. Our storm-battle for life brought him to light, and through him as through a window I have ever since been looking with deeper sympathy into all my fellow mortals." Accordingly, in the following essays Muir preached not only the theme of kinship, but also the need for a more respectful attitude toward domestic as well as wild animals.

Stickeen:
An Adventure
with a Dog
and a Glacier

I SET OFF EARLY THE MORNING OF AU-
gust 30 before any one else in camp had stirred, not waiting
for breakfast, but only eating a piece of bread. I had intended getting a cup of coffee, but a wild storm was blowing and calling, and I could not wait. Running out against
the rain-laden gale and turning to catch my breath, I saw
that the minister's little dog had left his bed in the tent and
was coming boring through the storm, evidently determined to follow me. I told him to go back, that such a day
as this had nothing for him.

"Go back," I shouted, "and get your breakfast." But he
simply stood with his head down, and when I began to urge
my way again, looking around, I saw he was still following
me. So I at last told him to come on if he must and gave
him a piece of the bread I had in my pocket.

* Domestic Animals *

Instead of falling, the rain, mixed with misty shreds of clouds, was flying in level sheets, and the wind was roaring as I had never heard wind roar before. Over the icy levels and over the woods, on the mountains, over the jagged rocks and spires and chasms of the glacier it boomed and moaned and roared, filling the fiord in even, gray, structureless gloom, inspiring and awful. I first struggled up in the face of the blast to the east end of the ice-wall, where a patch of forest had been carried away by the glacier when it was advancing. I noticed a few stumps well out on the moraine flat, showing that its present bare, raw condition was not the condition of fifty or a hundred years ago. In front of this part of the glacier there is a small moraine lake about half a mile in length, around the margin of which are a considerable number of trees standing knee-deep, and of course dead. This also is a result of the recent advance of the ice.

Pushing through the ragged edge of the woods on the left margin of the glacier, the storm seemed to increase in violence, so that it was difficult to draw breath in facing it; therefore I took shelter back of a tree to enjoy it and wait, hoping that it would at last somewhat abate. Here the glacier, descending over an abrupt rock, falls forward in grand cascades, while a stream swollen by the rain was now a torrent,—wind, rain, ice-torrent, and water-torrent in one grand symphony.

At length the storm seemed to abate somewhat, and I took off my heavy rubber boots, with which I had waded the glacial streams on the flat, and laid them with my overcoat on a log, where I might find them on my way back, knowing I would be drenched anyhow, and firmly tied my mountain shoes, tightened my belt, shouldered my ice-axe, and, thus free and ready for rough work, pushed on, regardless as possible of mere rain. Making my way up a steep granite slope, its projecting polished bosses encumbered here and there by boulders and the ground and bruised ruins of the ragged edge of the forest that had been uprooted by the glacier during its recent advance, I traced the side of the glacier for two or three miles, finding everywhere evidence of its having encroached on the woods, which here run back along its edge for fifteen or twenty miles. Under the projecting edge of this vast ice-river I could see down beneath it to a depth of fifty feet or so in some places, where logs and branches were being crushed to pulp, some of it almost fine enough for paper, though most of it stringy and coarse.

After thus tracing the margin of the glacier for three or four miles, I chopped steps and climbed to the top, and as far as the eye could reach, the nearly level glacier stretched indefinitely away in the gray cloudy sky, a prairie of ice. The wind was now almost moderate, though rain continued to fall, which I did not mind, but a tendency to mist in the drooping draggled clouds made me hesitate about attempting to cross to the opposite shore. Although the distance was only six or seven miles, no traces at this time could be seen of the mountains on the other side, and in case the sky should grow darker, as it seemed inclined to do, I feared that when I got out of sight of land and perhaps into a maze of crevasses I might find difficulty in winning a way back.

Lingering a while and sauntering about in sight of the shore, I found this eastern side of the glacier remarkably free from large crevasses. Nearly all I met were so narrow I could step across them almost anywhere, while the few wide ones were easily avoided by going up or down along their sides to where they narrowed. The dismal cloud ceiling showed rifts here and there, and, thus encouraged, I struck out for the west shore, aiming to strike it five or six miles above the front wall, cautiously taking compass bearings at short intervals to enable me to find my way back should the weather darken again with mist or rain or snow. The structure lines of the glacier itself were, however, my main guide. All went well. I came to a deeply furrowed section about two miles in width where I had to zigzag in long, tedious tacks and make narrow doublings, tracing the edges of wide longitudinal furrows and chasms until I could find a bridge connecting their sides, oftentimes making the direct distance ten times over. The walking was good of its kind, however, and by dint of patient doubling and axe-work on dangerous places, I gained the opposite shore in about three hours, the width of the glacier at this point being about seven miles. Occasionally, while making my way, the clouds lifted a little, revealing a few bald, rough mountains sunk to the throat in the broad, icy sea which encompassed them on all sides, sweeping on forever and forever as we count time, wearing them away, giving them the shape they are destined to take when in the fullness of time they shall be parts of new landscapes.

Ere I lost sight of the east-side mountains, those on the west came in sight, so that holding my course was easy, and, though making haste, I halted for a moment to gaze down into the beautiful pure blue crevasses and to drink at the lovely blue wells, the most beautiful of all Nature's water-basins, or at the rills and streams outspread over the ice-land prairie, never ceasing to admire their lovely color and music as they glided and swirled in their blue crystal channels and potholes, and the rumbling of the moulins, or mills, where streams poured into blue-walled pits of unknown depth, some of them as regularly circular as if bored with augers. Interesting, too, were the cascades over blue cliffs, where streams fell into crevasses or slid almost noiselessly down slopes so smooth and frictionless their motion was concealed. The round or oval wells, however, from one to ten feet wide, and from one to twenty or thirty feet deep, were perhaps the most beautiful of all, the water so pure as to be almost invisible. My widest views did not probably exceed fifteen miles, the rain and mist making distances seem greater.

On reaching the farther shore and tracing it a few miles to northward, I found a large portion of the glacier-current sweeping out westward in a bold and beautiful curve around the shoulder of a mountain as if going direct to the open sea. Leaving the main trunk, it breaks into a magnificent uproar of pinnacles and spires and up-heaving, splashing wave-shaped masses, a crystal cataract incomparably greater and wilder than a score of Niagaras.

Tracing its channel three or four miles, I found that it fell into a lake, which it fills with bergs. The front of this branch of the glacier is about three miles wide. I first took the lake to be the head of an arm of the sea, but, going down to its shore and tasting it, I found it fresh, and by my aneroid perhaps less than a hundred feet above sea-level. It is probably separated from the sea only by a moraine dam. I had not time to go around its shores, as it was now near five o'clock and I was about fifteen miles from camp, and I had to make haste to recross the glacier before dark, which would come on about eight o'clock. I therefore made haste up to the main glacier, and, shaping my course by compass and the structure lines of the ice, set off from the land out on to the grand crystal prairie again. All was so silent and so concentred, owing to the low dragging mist, the beauty close about me was all the more keenly felt, though tinged with a dim sense of danger, as if coming events were casting shadows. I was soon out of sight of land, and the evening dusk that on cloudy days precedes the real night gloom came stealing on and only ice was in sight, and the only sounds, save the low rumbling of the mills and the rattle of falling stones at long intervals, were the low, terribly earnest moanings of the wind or distant waterfalls coming through the thickening gloom. After two hours of hard work I came to a maze of crevasses of appalling depth and width which could not be passed apparently either up or down. I traced them with firm nerve developed by the danger, making wide jumps, poising cautiously on dizzy edges after cutting footholds, taking wide crevasses at a grand leap at once frightful and inspiring. Many a mile was thus traveled, mostly up and down the glacier, making but little real headway, running much of the time as the danger of having to pass the night on the ice became more and more imminent. This I could do, though with the weather and my rain-soaked condition it would be trying at best. In treading the mazes of this crevassed section I had frequently to cross bridges that were only knife-edges for twenty or thirty feet, cutting off the sharp tops and leaving them flat so that little Stickeen could follow me. These I had to straddle, cutting off the top as I progressed and hitching gradually ahead like a boy riding a rail fence. All this time the little dog followed me bravely, never hesitating on the brink of any crevasse that I had jumped, but now that it was becoming dark and the crevasses became more troublesome, he followed close at my heels instead of scampering far and wide, where the ice was at all smooth, as he had in the forenoon. No land was now in sight. The mist fell lower and darker and snow began to fly. I could not see far enough up and down the glacier to judge how best to work out of the bewildering labyrinth, and how hard I tried while there was yet hope of reaching camp that night! a hope which was fast growing dim like the sky. After dark, on such ground, to keep from freezing, I could only jump up and down until morning on a piece of flat ice between the crevasses, dance to the boding music of the winds and waters, and as I was already tired and hungry I would be in bad condition for such ice work. Many times I was put to my mettle, but with a firm-braced nerve, all the more unflinching as the dangers thickened, I worked out of that terrible ice-web, and with blood fairly up Stickeen and I ran over common danger without fatigue. Our very hardest trial was in getting across the very last of the sliver bridges. After examining the first of the two widest crevasses, I followed its edge half a mile or so up and down and discovered that its narrowest spot was about eight feet wide, which was the limit of what I was able to jump. Moreover, the side I was on—that is, the west side—was about a foot higher than the other, and I feared that in case I should be stopped by a still wider impassable crevasse ahead that I would hardly be able to take back that jump from its lower side. The ice beyond, however, as far as I could see it, looked temptingly smooth. Therefore, after carefully making a socket for my foot on the rounded brink, I jumped, but found that I had nothing to spare and more than ever dreaded having to retrace my way. Little Stickeen jumped this, however, without apparently taking a second look at it, and we ran ahead joyfully over smooth, level ice, hoping we were now leaving all danger behind us. But hardly had we gone a hundred or two yards when to our dismay we found ourselves on the very widest of all the longitudinal crevasses we had yet encountered. It was about forty feet wide. I ran anxiously up the side of it to northward, eagerly hoping that I could get around its head, but my worst fears were realized when at a distance of about

a mile or less it ran into the crevasse that I had just jumped.
I then ran down the edge for a mile or more below the point
where I had first met it, and found that its lower end also
united with the crevasse I had jumped, showing dismally
that we were on an island two or three hundred yards wide
and about two miles long and the only way of escape from
this island was by turning back and jumping again that
crevasse which I dreaded, or venturing ahead across the
giant crevasse by the very worst of the sliver bridges I had
ever seen. It was so badly weathered and melted down that
it formed a knife-edge, and extended across from side to
side in a low, drooping curve like that made by a loose rope
attached at each end at the same height. But the worst difficulty was that the ends of the down-curving sliver were
attached to the sides at a depth of about eight or ten feet
below the surface of the glacier. Getting down to the end of
the bridge, and then after crossing it getting up the other
side, seemed hardly possible. However, I decided to dare
the dangers of the fearful sliver rather than to attempt to
retrace my steps. Accordingly I dug a low groove in the
rounded edge for my knees to rest in and, leaning over,
began to cut a narrow foothold on the steep, smooth side.
When I was doing this, Stickeen came up behind me,
pushed his head over my shoulder, looked into the crevasses
and along the narrow knife-edge, then turned and looked
in my face, muttering and whining as if trying to say,
"Surely you are not going down there." I said, "Yes, Stickeen, this is the only way." He then began to cry and ran

wildly along the rim of the crevasse, searching for a better way, then, returning baffled, of course, he came behind me and lay down and cried louder and louder.

After getting down one step I cautiously stooped and cut another and another in succession until I reached the point where the sliver was attached to the wall. There, cautiously balancing, I chipped down the upcurved end of the bridge until I had formed a small level platform about a foot wide, then, bending forward, got astride of the end of the sliver, steadied myself with my knees, then cut off the top of the sliver, hitching myself forward an inch or two at a time, leaving it about four inches wide for Stickeen. Arrived at the farther end of the sliver, which was about seventy-five feet long, I chipped another little platform on its upcurved end, cautiously rose to my feet, and with infinite pains cut narrow notch steps and finger-holds in the wall and finally got safely across. All this dreadful time poor little Stickeen was crying as if his heart was broken, and when I called to him in as reassuring a voice as I could muster, he only cried the louder, as if trying to say that he never, never could get down there—the only time that the brave little fellow appeared to know what danger was. After going away as if I was leaving him, he still howled and cried without venturing to try to follow me. Returning to the edge of the crevasse, I told him that I must go, that he could come if he only tried, and finally in despair he hushed his cries, slid his little feet slowly down into my footsteps out on the big sliver, walked slowly and cautiously along the sliver as if holding his breath, while the snow was falling and the wind

was moaning and threatening to blow him off. When he
arrived at the foot of the slope below me, I was kneeling on
the brink ready to assist him in case he should be unable to
reach the top. He looked up along the row of notched steps
I had made, as if fixing them in his mind, then with a
nervous spring he whizzed up and passed me out on to the
level ice, and ran and cried and barked and rolled about
fairly hysterical in the sudden revulsion from the depth of
despair to triumphant joy. I tried to catch him and pet him
and tell him how good and brave he was, but he would not
be caught. He ran round and round, swirling like autumn
leaves in an eddy, lay down and rolled head over heels. I
told him we still had far to go and that we must now stop all
nonsense and get off the ice before dark. I knew by the ice-
lines that every step was now taking me nearer the shore
and soon it came in sight. The headland four or five miles
back from the front, covered with spruce trees, loomed
faintly but surely through the mist and light fall of snow
not more than two miles away. The ice now proved good all
the way across, and we reached the lateral moraine just at
dusk, then with trembling limbs, now that the danger was
over, we staggered and stumbled down the bouldery edge
of the glacier and got over the dangerous rocks by the cascades while yet a faint light lingered. We were safe, and
then, too, came limp weariness such as no ordinary work
ever produces, however hard it may be. Wearily we stumbled down through the woods, over logs and brush and
roots, devil's-clubs pricking us at every faint blundering
tumble. At last we got out on the smooth mud slope with

only a mile of slow but sure dragging of weary limbs to camp. The Indians had been firing guns to guide me and had a fine supper and fire ready, though fearing they would be compelled to seek us in the morning, a care not often applied to me. Stickeen and I were too tired to eat much, and, strange to say, too tired to sleep. Both of us, springing up in the night again and again, fancied we were still on that dreadful ice bridge in the shadow of death.

Nevertheless, we arose next morning in newness of life. Never before had rocks and ice and trees seemed so beautiful and wonderful, even the cold, biting rainstorm that was blowing seemed full of loving-kindness, wonderful compensation for all that we had endured, and we sailed down the bay through the gray, driving rain rejoicing.

Cats and Dogs

SOON AFTER OUR ARRIVAL IN THE WOODS some one added a cat and puppy to the animals father had bought.* The cat soon had kittens, and it was interesting to watch her feeding, protecting, and training them. After they were able to leave their nest and play, she went out hunting and brought in many kinds of birds and squirrels for them, mostly ground squirrels (spermophiles), called "gophers" in Wisconsin. When she got within a dozen yards or so of the shanty, she announced her approach by a peculiar call, and the sleeping kittens immediately bounced up and ran to meet her, all racing for the first bite of they knew not what, and we too ran to see what she brought. She then lay down a few minutes to rest and enjoy

*Muir and his family had moved from Dunbar, Scotland, to Wisconsin when he was eleven.

95

the enjoyment of her feasting family, and again vanished in the grass and flowers, coming and going every half-hour or so. Sometimes she brought in birds that we had never seen before, and occasionally a flying squirrel, chipmunk, or big fox squirrel. We were just old enough, David and I, to regard all these creatures as wonders, the strange inhabitants of our new world.

The pup was a common cur, though very uncommon to us, a black and white short-haired mongrel that we named "Watch." We always gave him a pan of milk in the evening just before we knelt in family worship, while daylight still lingered in the shanty. And, instead of attending to the prayers, I too often studied the small wild creatures playing around us. Field mice scampered about the cabin as though it had been built for them alone, and their performances were very amusing. About dusk, on one of the calm, sultry nights so grateful to moths and beetles, when the puppy was lapping his milk, and we were on our knees, in through the door came a heavy broad-shouldered beetle about as big as a mouse, and after it had droned and boomed round the cabin two or three times, the pan of milk, showing white in the gloaming, caught its eyes, and, taking good aim, it alighted with a slanting, glinting plash in the middle of the pan like a duck alighting in a lake. Baby Watch, having never before seen anything like that beetle, started back, gazing in dumb astonishment and fear at the black sprawling monster trying to swim. Recovering somewhat from his fright, he began to bark at the creature, and ran round and round his milk-pan, wouf-woufing, gurring, growling, like an old dog barking at a wild-cat or a bear. The natural astonishment and curiosity of that boy dog getting his first entomological lesson in this wonderful world was so immoderately funny that I had great difficulty in keeping from laughing out loud.

Snapping turtles were common throughout the woods, and we were delighted to find that they would snap at a stick and hang on like bull-dogs; and we amused ourselves by introducing Watch to them, enjoying his curious behavior and theirs in getting acquainted with each other. One day we assisted one of the smallest of the turtles to get a good grip of poor Watch's ear. Then away he rushed, holding his head sidewise, yelping and terror-stricken, with the strange buglike reptile biting hard and clinging fast—a shameful amusement even for wild boys.

As a playmate Watch was too serious, though he learned more than any stranger would judge him capable of, was a bold, faithful watch-dog, and in his prime a grand fighter, able to whip all the other dogs in the neighborhood. Comparing him with ourselves, we soon learned that although he could not read books he could read faces, was a good judge of character, always knew what was going on and what we were about to do, and liked to help us. We could run nearly as fast as he could, see about as far, and perhaps hear as well, but in sense of smell his nose was incomparably better than ours. One sharp winter morning when the ground was covered with snow, I noticed that when he was yawning and stretching himself after leaving his bed he suddenly caught the scent of something that excited him, went round the corner of the house, and looked intently to the westward across a tongue of land that we called West Bank, eagerly questioning the air with quivering nostrils, and bristling up as though he felt sure that there was something dangerous in that direction and had actually caught sight of it. Then he ran toward the Bank, and I followed him, curious to see what his nose had discovered. The top of the Bank commanded a view of the north end of our lake and meadow, and when we got there we saw an Indian hunter with a long spear, going from one muskrat cabin to another, approaching cautiously, careful to make no noise, and then suddenly thrusting his spear down through the house. If well aimed, the spear went through the poor beaver rat as it lay cuddled up in the snug nest it had made for itself in the fall with so much far-seeing care, and when the hunter felt the spear quivering, he dug down the mossy hut with his tomahawk and secured his prey,—the flesh for food, and the skin to sell for a dime or so. This was a clear object lesson on dogs' keenness of scent. That Indian was more than half a mile away across a wooded ridge. Had the hunter been a white man, I suppose Watch would not have noticed him.

When he was about six or seven years old, he not only became cross, so that he would do only what he liked, but he fell on evil ways, and was accused by the neighbors who had settled around us of catching and devouring whole broods of chickens, some of them only a day or two out of the shell. We never imagined he would do anything so grossly undoglike. He never did at home. But several of the neighbors declared over and over again that they had caught him in the act, and insisted that he must be shot. At last, in spite of tearful protests, he was condemned and executed. Father examined the poor fellow's stomach in search of sure evidence, and discovered the heads of eight chickens that he had devoured at his last meal. So poor Watch was killed simply because his taste for chickens was too much like our own. Think of the millions of squabs that preaching, praying men and women kill and eat, with all sorts of other animals great and small, young and old, while eloquently discoursing on the coming of the blessed peaceful, bloodless millennium! Think of the passenger pigeons that fifty or sixty years ago filled the woods and sky over half the continent, now exterminated by beating down the young from the nests together with the brooding parents, before they could try their wonderful wings; by trapping them in nets, feeding them to hogs, etc. None of our fellow mortals is safe who eats what we eat, who in any way interferes with our pleasures, or who may be used for work or food, clothing or ornament, or mere cruel, sportish amusement. Fortunately many are too small to be seen, and therefore enjoy life beyond our reach. And in looking through God's great stone books made up of records reaching back millions and millions of years, it is a great comfort to learn that vast multitudes of creatures, great and small and infinite in number, lived and had a good time in God's love before man was created.

Horses

AS I WAS THE ELDEST BOY I HAD THE care of our first span of work horses. Their names were Nob and Nell. Nob was very intelligent, and even affectionate, and could learn almost anything. Nell was entirely different; balky and stubborn, though we managed to teach her a good many circus tricks; but she never seemed to like to play with us in anything like an affectionate way as Nob did. We turned them out one day into the pasture, and an Indian, hiding in the brush that had sprung up after the grass fires had been kept out, managed to catch Nob, tied a rope to her jaw for a bridle, rode her to Green Lake, about thirty or forty miles away, and tried to sell her for fifteen dollars. All our hearts were sore, as if one of the family had been lost. We hunted everywhere and could not at first

Horses

imagine what had become of her. We discovered her track where the fence was broken down, and, following it for a few miles, made sure the track was Nob's; and a neighbor told us he had seen an Indian riding fast through the woods on a horse that looked like Nob. But we could find no farther trace of her until a month or two after she was lost, and we had given up hope of ever seeing her again. Then we learned that she had been taken from an Indian by a farmer at Green Lake because he saw that she had been shod and had worked in harness. So when the Indian tried to sell her the farmer said: "You are a thief. That is a white man's horse. You stole her."

"No," said the Indian, "I bought her from Prairie du Chien and she has always been mine."

The man, pointing to her feet and the marks of the harness, said: "You are lying. I will take that horse away from you and put her in my pasture, and if you come near it I will set the dogs on you." Then he advertised her. One of our neighbors happened to see the advertisement and brought us the glad news, and great was our rejoicing when father brought her home. That Indian must have treated her with terrible cruelty, for when I was riding her through the pasture several years afterward, looking for another horse that we wanted to catch, as we approached the place where she had been captured she stood stock still gazing through the bushes, fearing the Indian might still be hiding there ready to spring; and she was so excited that she trembled, and her heartbeats were so loud that I could hear

101

them distinctly as I sat on her back, *boomp, boomp, boomp,* like the drumming of a partridge. So vividly had she remembered her terrible experiences.

She was a great pet and favorite with the whole family, quickly learned playful tricks, came running when we called, seemed to know everything we said to her, and had the utmost confidence in our friendly kindness.

We used to cut and shock and husk the Indian corn in the fall, until a keen Yankee stopped overnight at our house and among other labor-saving notions convinced father that it was better to let it stand, and husk it at his leisure during the winter, then turn in the cattle to eat the leaves and trample down the stalks, so that they could be ploughed under in the spring. In this winter method each of us took two rows and husked into baskets, and emptied the corn on the ground in piles of fifteen to twenty basketfuls, then loaded it into the wagon to be hauled to the crib. This was cold, painful work, the temperature being oftentimes far below zero and the ground covered with dry, frosty snow, giving rise to miserable crops of chilblains and frosted fingers—a sad change from the merry Indian-summer husking, when the big yellow pumpkins covered the cleared fields; —golden corn, golden pumpkins, gathered in the hazy golden weather. Sad change, indeed, but we occasionally got some fun out of the nipping, shivery work from hungry prairie chickens, and squirrels and mice that came about us.

The piles of corn were often left in the field several days, and while loading them into the wagon we usually found field mice in them, —big, blunt-nosed, strong-scented fellows that we were taught to kill just because they nibbled a few grains of corn. I used to hold one while it was still warm, up to Nob's nose for the fun of seeing her make faces and snort at the smell of it; and I would say: "Here, Nob," as if offering her a lump of sugar. One day I offered her an extra fine, fat, plump specimen, something like a little woodchuck, or muskrat, and to my astonishment, after smelling it curiously and doubtfully, as if wondering what the gift might be, and rubbing it back and forth in the palm of my hand with her upper lip, she deliberately took it into her mouth, crunched and munched and chewed it fine and swallowed it, bones, teeth, head, tail, everything. Not a single hair of that mouse was wasted. When she was chewing it she nodded and grunted, as though critically tasting and relishing it.

My father was a steadfast enthusiast on religious matters, and, of course, attended almost every sort of church-meeting, especially revival meetings. They were occasionally held in summer, but mostly in winter when the sleighing was good and plenty of time available. One hot summer day father drove Nob to Portage and back, twenty-four miles over a sandy road. It was a hot, hard, sultry day's work, and she had evidently been over-driven in order to get home in time for one of these meetings. I shall never forget how tired and wilted she looked that evening when I unhitched her; how she drooped in her stall, too

tired to eat or even to lie down. Next morning it was plain
that her lungs were inflamed; all the dreadful symptoms
were just the same as my own when I had pneumonia. Father sent for a Methodist minister, a very energetic, resourceful man, who was a blacksmith, farmer, butcher,
and horse-doctor as well as minister; but all his gifts and
skill were of no avail. Nob was doomed. We bathed her
head and tried to get her to eat something, but she could n't
eat, and in about a couple of weeks we turned her loose to
let her come around the house and see us in the weary suffering and loneliness of the shadow of death. She tried to
follow us children, so long her friends and workmates and
playmates. It was awfully touching. She had several hem-
orrhages, and in the forenoon of her last day, after she had
had one of her dreadful spells of bleeding and gasping for
breath, she came to me trembling, with beseeching, heart-
breaking looks, and after I had bathed her head and tried
to soothe and pet her, she lay down and gasped and died.
All the family gathered about her, weeping, with aching
hearts. Then dust to dust.

She was the most faithful, intelligent, playful, affectionate, human-like horse I ever knew, and she won all our
hearts. Of the many advantages of farm life for boys one of
the greatest is the gaining a real knowledge of animals as
fellow-mortals, learning to respect them and love them,
and even to win some of their love. Thus godlike sympathy
grows and thrives and spreads far beyond the teachings of
churches and schools, where too often the mean, blinding,

* Horses *

loveless doctrine is taught that animals have neither mind nor soul, have no rights that we are bound to respect, and were made only for man, to be petted, spoiled, slaughtered, or enslaved.

CHAPTER FOUR

✳

INSECTS

Although he wrote primarily about large and spectacular animals, John Muir urged readers to observe the small and seemingly insignificant as well. Compared with insects, "Godlike man's greatest machines are as nothing," reads a passage in My First Summer in the Sierra. *Accordingly, Muir found such traditionally distasteful subjects as flies and mosquitoes to be worthy of consideration. Even the unusually perverse and savage black ant was to him a "wonderful electric species." The following essays demonstrate his considerable enthusiasm for the insect world.*

The Grasshopper

A QUEER FELLOW AND A JOLLY FEL-
low is the grasshopper. Up the mountains he comes on
excursions, how high I don't know, but at least as far and
high as Yosemite tourists. I was much interested with the
hearty enjoyment of the one that danced and sang for me on
the Dome this afternoon. He seemed brimful of glad, hilarious energy, manifested by springing into the air to a
height of twenty or thirty feet, then diving and springing
up again and making a sharp musical rattle just as the lowest point in the descent was reached. Up and down a dozen
times or so he danced and sang, then alighted to rest, then
up and at it again. The curves he described in the air in
diving and rattling resembled those made by cords hanging loosely and attached at the same height at the ends, the
loops nearly covering each other. Braver, heartier, keener,

care-free enjoyment of life I have never seen or heard in
any creature, great or small. The life of this comic red-
legs, the mountain's merriest child, seems to be made up of
pure, condensed gayety. The Douglas squirrel is the only
living creature that I can compare him with in exuberant,
rollicking, irrepressible jollity. Wonderful that these sublime mountains are so loudly cheered and brightened by a
creature so queer. Nature in him seems to be snapping her
fingers in the face of all earthly dejection and melancholy
with a boyish hip-hip-hurrah. How the sound is made I do
not understand. When he was on the ground he made not
the slightest noise, nor when he was simply flying from
place to place, but only when diving in curves, the motion
seeming to be required for the sound; for the more vigorous the diving the more energetic the corresponding out-
bursts of jolly rattling. I tried to observe him closely while
he was resting in the intervals of his performances; but he
would not allow a near approach, always getting his jumping legs ready to spring for immediate flight, and keeping
his eyes on me. A fine sermon the little fellow danced for
me on the Dome, a likely place to look for sermons in
stones, but not for grasshopper sermons. A large and imposing pulpit for so small a preacher. No danger of weak-
ness in the knees of the world while Nature can spring such
a rattle as this. Even the bear did not express for me the
mountain's wild health and strength and happiness so tell-
ingly as did this comical little hopper. No cloud of care in
his day, no winter of discontent in sight. To him every day

* The Grasshopper *

is a holiday; and when at length his sun sets, I fancy he will cuddle down on the forest floor and die like the leaves and flowers, and like them leave no unsightly remains calling for burial.

Ants

MASTODONS AND ELEPHANTS USED TO
live here no great geological time ago, as shown by their
bones, often discovered by miners in washing gold-gravel.
And bears of at least two species are here now, besides the
California lion or panther, and wild cats, wolves, foxes,
snakes, scorpions, wasps, tarantulas; but one is almost
tempted at times to regard a small savage black ant as the
master existence of this vast mountain world. These fear-
less, restless, wandering imps, though only about a quarter
of an inch long, are fonder of fighting and biting than any
beast I know. They attack every living thing around their
homes, often without cause as far as I can see. Their bodies
are mostly jaws curved like ice-hooks, and to get work for
these weapons seems to be their chief aim and pleasure.
Most of their colonies are established in living oaks some-

what decayed or hollowed, in which they can conveniently build their cells. These are chosen probably because of their strength as opposed to the attacks of animals and storms. They work both day and night, creep into dark caves, climb the highest trees, wander and hunt through cool ravines as well as on hot, unshaded ridges, and extend their highways and byways over everything but water and sky. From the foothills to a mile above the level of the sea nothing can stir without their knowledge; and alarms are spread in an incredibly short time, without any howl or cry that we can hear. I can't understand the need of their ferocious courage; there seems to be no common sense in it. Sometimes, no doubt, they fight in defense of their homes, but they fight anywhere and always wherever they can find anything to bite. As soon as a vulnerable spot is discovered on man or beast, they stand on their heads and sink their jaws, and though torn limb from limb, they will yet hold on and die biting deeper. When I contemplate this fierce creature so widely distributed and strongly intrenched, I see that much remains to be done ere the world is brought under the rule of universal peace and love.

On my way to camp a few minutes ago, I passed a dead pine nearly ten feet in diameter. It has been enveloped in fire from top to bottom so that now it looks like a grand black pillar set up as a monument. In this noble shaft a colony of large jet-black ants have established themselves, laboriously cutting tunnels and cells through the wood, whether sound or decayed. The entire trunk seems to have been honeycombed, judging by the size of the talus of gnawed chips like sawdust piled up around its base. They are more intelligent looking than their small, belligerent, strong-scented brethren, and have better manners, though quick to fight when required. Their towns are carved in fallen trunks as well as in those left standing, but never in sound, living trees or in the ground. When you happen to sit down to rest or take notes near a colony, some wandering hunter is sure to find you and come cautiously forward to discover the nature of the intruder and what ought to be done. If you are not too near the town and keep perfectly still he may run across your feet a few times, over your legs and hands and face, up your trousers, as if taking your measure and getting comprehensive views, then go in peace without raising an alarm. If, however, a tempting spot is offered or some suspicious movement excites him, a bite follows, and such a bite! I fancy that a bear or wolf bite is not to be compared with it. A quick electric flame of pain flashes along the outraged nerves, and you discover for the first time how great is the capacity for sensation you are possessed of. A shriek, a grab for the animal, and a bewildered stare follow this bite of bites as one comes back to consciousness from sudden eclipse. Fortunately, if careful, one need not be bitten oftener than once or twice in a lifetime. This wonderful electric species is about three fourths of an inch long. Bears are fond of them, and tear and gnaw their home-logs to pieces, and roughly devour the eggs, larvæ, parent ants, and the rotten or sound wood of the cells, all in one spicy acid hash. The Digger Indians also are fond of the larvæ and even of the perfect ants, so I have been told by old mountaineers. They bite off and reject the head, and eat the tickly acid body with keen relish. Thus are the poor biters bitten, like every other biter, big or little, in the world's great family.

There is also a fine, active, intelligent-looking red species, intermediate in size between the above. They dwell in the ground, and build large piles of seed husks, leaves, straw, etc., over their nests. Their food seems to be mostly insects and plant leaves, seeds and sap. How many mouths Nature has to fill, how many neighbors we have, how little we know about them, and how seldom we get in each other's way! Then to think of the infinite numbers of smaller fellow mortals, invisibly small, compared with which the smallest ants are as mastodons.

The
Bee-Pastures
of California

PART ONE

WHEN CALIFORNIA WAS WILD, IT WAS
one sweet bee-garden throughout its entire length, north
and south, and all the way across from the snowy sierra to
the ocean.

Wherever a bee might fly within the bounds of this vir-
gin wilderness—through the redwood forests, along the
banks of the rivers, along the bluffs and headlands fronting
the sea, over valley and plain, park and grove, and deep
leafy glen, or far up the piney slopes of the mountains—
throughout every belt and section of climate, bee flowers
bloomed in lavish abundance. Here they grew more or less
apart in special sheets and patches of no great size, there in
broad, flowing folds hundreds of miles in length, zones of
polleny forests, zones of flowery chaparral, stream-tangles

of rubus and wild rose, sheets of golden compositæ, beds of violets, beds of mint, beds of bryanthus and clover, and so on, certain species blooming somewhere around all the year.

But of late years plow and sheep have made sad havoc in these glorious pastures, destroying tens of thousands of the flowery acres like a fire, and banishing many species of the best honey-plants to rocky cliffs and fence corners, while, on the other hand, culture thus far has given no adequate compensation, at least in kind—acres of alfalfa for miles of the richest wild pasture, ornamental roses and honey-suckles around cottage doors for cascades of wild roses in the dells, and small, square orchards and orange-groves for broad mountain-belts of chaparral.

Only ten years ago, the Great Central Plain of California, during the months of March, April, and May, was one smooth, continuous bed of honey-bloom, so marvelously rich that, in walking from one end of it to the other, a distance of more than four hundred miles, your feet would press more than a hundred flowers at every step. Mints, gilias, nemophilas, castilleias, and innumerable compositæ were so crowded together that, had ninety-nine in every hundred been taken away, the plain would still have seemed extravagantly flowery to any but Californians. The radiant, honeyful corollas, touching and over-lapping, and rising above one another, glowed in the living light like a sunset sky—one glorious blaze of purple and gold. Down through the midst flowed many a river, the Sacramento from the north, the San Joaquin from the south, with noble tributaries sweeping in at right angles from the mountains, dividing the plain into sections fringed with trees.

Along each river and tributary there is a strip of bottom-land, countersunk beneath the general level, and wider toward the foot-hills, where magnificent oaks, from three to eight feet in diameter, cast grateful masses of shade over the open, prairie-like level. And close along the water's edge there is a fine jungle of tropical luxuriance, composed of wild rose and bramble bushes and a great variety of climbing vines, wreathing and interlacing the branches and trunks of willows and alders, and swinging across from summit to summit in heavy festoons. Here the wild bees revel in fresh bloom long after the flowers of the drier plain have withered and gone to seed. And in midsummer, when the "blackberries" are ripe, the Indians come from the mountains to feast—men, women, and babies in long, noisy trains, oftentimes joined by the farmers of the neighborhood, who gather this wild fruit with commendable appreciation of its superior flavor, while their home orchards are full of ripe peaches, apricots, nectarines, and figs, and their vineyards are laden with grapes. But, though these luxuriant bottoms are thus distinct from the smooth, treeless plain, they make no heavy dividing lines in general views. The whole appears as one continuous sheet of bloom, bounded only by the mountains.

My first view of this central garden, the most extensive and best defined of all the bee-pastures of the State, was

* The Bee-Pastures of California *

obtained from the summit of the Pacheco pass, about the middle of April, 1868, when it was rejoicing in all its glory. Along the eastern horizon rose the mighty sierra, white and jagged with snowy peaks along the top, dark with forests in the middle region, and purple with grasses and flowers and chaparral at the base, and blending gracefully in smooth hill undulations into the glowing yellow plain, which, like a cloth of gold, was seen flowing away to north and south as far as the eye could reach: hazy and vanishing in the distance, distinct as a new map along the foot-hills at my feet—the sunny sky arching over all.

Descending the eastern slopes of the coast range, through beds of gilias and lupines, and around many a breezy hillock and bush-crowned headland, I at length waded out into the midst of the glorious field of gold. All the ground was covered, not with grass and green leaves, but with radiant corollas, about ankle-deep next the foot-hills, knee-deep or more five or six miles out. Here were bahia, madia, madaria, burrielia, chrysopsis, corethrogyne, grindelia, etc., growing in close social congregations of various shades of yellow, blending finely with the purples of clarkia, orthocarpus, and œnothera, whose delicate petals were drinking the vital sunbeams without giving back any sparkling glow.

Because so long a period of extreme drought succeeds the rainy season, most of the vegetation is composed of annuals, which spring up simultaneously and bloom together at about the same height above the ground, the general surface being but slightly ruffled by the taller phacelias, pentstemons, and groups of *Salvia carduacea*, the king of the mints.

Sauntering in any direction, hundreds of these happy sun-plants brushed against my feet at every step, and closed over them as if I were wading in liquid gold. The air was sweet with fragrance, the larks sang their blessed songs, rising on the wing as I advanced, then sinking out of sight in the polleny sod, while myriads of wild bees stirred the lower air with their monotonous hum—monotonous, yet forever fresh and sweet as every-day sunshine. Hares and spermophiles showed themselves in considerable numbers, and small bands of antelope were almost constantly in sight, gazing curiously from some slight elevation, and then bounding swiftly away with unrivaled grace of motion. Yet I could discover no crushed flowers to mark their track, nor, indeed, any destructive action of any wild foot or tooth whatever.

The great yellow days circled by uncounted, while I drifted toward the north, observing the countless forms of life thronging about me—lying down almost anywhere on the approach of night. And what glorious botanical beds I had! Oftentimes on awaking I would find several new species leaning over me and looking me full in the face, so that my studies would begin before rising.

About the first of May I turned eastward, crossing the San Joaquin between the mouths of the Tuolumne and Merced, and by the time I had reached the Sierra foothills, most of the vegetation had gone to seed and become as dry as hay.

All the seasons of the great plain are warm or temperate, and bee-flowers are never wholly wanting; but the grand springtime—the annual resurrection—is governed by the rains, which usually set in about the middle of December or the beginning of January. Then the seeds, that for six months have lain on the ground dry and fresh as if they had been gathered into barns, at once unfold their treasured life. The general brown and purple of the ground, and the dead vegetation of the preceding year, give place to the green of mosses and liverworts and myriads of young leaves. Then one species after another comes into flower, gradually overspreading the green with yellow and purple, which lasts until May.

The "rainy season" is by no means a gloomy, soggy period of constant cloudiness and rain. Nowhere else in North America, perhaps in the world, are the months of December, January, February, and March so full of bland, plant-building sunshine. Referring to my notes of the winter and spring of 1868–9, every day of which I spent out of doors, on that section of the plain lying between the Tuolumne and Merced rivers, I find that the first rain of the season fell on the 18th of December. January had only six rainy days—that is, days on which rain fell; February three, March five, April three, and May three, completing the so-called rainy season, which was about an average one. The ordinary rain-storm of this region is seldom very cold or violent. The winds, which in settled weather come from the north-east, veer round into the opposite direction, the sky fills gradually and evenly with one general cloud, from which the rain falls steadily, often for several days in succession, at a temperature of about 45° or 50°.

More than seventy-five per cent of all the rain of this season came from the south-east. One magnificent storm from the north-west fell on the 21st of March. A massive, round-browed cloud came swelling and thundering over the flowery plain in most imposing majesty, its bossy front burning white and purple in the full blaze of the sun, while warm rain poured from its ample fountains like a cataract, beating down flowers and bees, and flooding the dry water-courses as suddenly as those of Nevada are flooded by "cloud-bursts." But in less than half an hour not a trace of the heavy mountain-like cloud-structure was left in the sky, and the bees were on the wing as if nothing more gratefully refreshing could have been sent them.

By the end of January four plants were in flower, and five or six mosses had already adjusted their hoods and were in the prime of life, but the flowers were not sufficiently numerous to affect greatly the general green of the young leaves. Violets made their appearance on the first week of February, and toward the end of this month the warmer portions of the plain were already golden with myriads of the flowers of rayed compositæ.

This was the full spring-time. New species bloomed every day. The sunshine grew warmer and richer. The air became more tuneful from day to day with humming

wings, and sweeter with the fragrance of the opening flowers. Ants were getting ready for their summer work, rubbing their benumbed limbs, and sunning themselves on
the husk-piles before their doors, and spiders were busy
mending their old webs or weaving new ones.

In March, vegetation was more than doubled in depth
and splendor; claytonia, calandrinia, a large white gilia,
and two nemophilas were in bloom, together with a host of
yellow compositæ, tall enough to bend in the wind and
show wavering ripples of shade.

In April, plant-life as a whole reached its greatest
height, and the plain over all its varied surface was mantled
with a close furred plush of purple and golden corollas. By
the end of this month most of the species had ripened their
seeds, but undecayed, still seemed to be in bloom from the
numerous corolla-like involucres and whorls of chaffy
scales of the compositæ. In May the bees found only a few
deep-set liliaceous plants and eriogonums in flower.

June, July, August, and September was the season of
rest and sleep,—the winter of dry heat,—followed in Oc-
tober by a second outburst of bloom at the very driest time
of the year. Then, after the shrunken mass of leaves and
stalks of the dead vegetation crinkle and turn to dust beneath the foot, as if it had been baked in an oven, *Hemizonia
virgata*, a slender, unobtrusive little plant, from six inches
to three feet high, suddenly makes its appearance in patches
miles in extent, like a resurrection of the bloom of April. I
have counted upward of three thousand flowers, five-
eighths of an inch in diameter, on a single plant. Both

leaves and stems are so slender as to be nearly invisible amid so showy a multitude of flowers. The ray and disk flowers are both yellow, the stamens purple, the texture of the rays being rich and velvety, like the petals of garden pansies. The prevailing wind turns all the heads round to the south-east, so that in facing north-westward we have the flowers looking us in the face. In our estimation, this little plant, the last-born of the brilliant host of compositæ that glorify the plain, is the most interesting of all. It remains in flower until November, uniting with two or three species of wiry eriogonums, which continue the floral chain around December to the spring flowers of January. Thus, although the main bloom and honey season is only about three months long, the floral circle, however thin around some of the hot, rainless months, is never completely broken.

How long the various species of wild bees have lived in this honey-garden nobody knows; probably ever since the main body of the present flora gained possession of the land, toward the close of the glacial period. The first brown honey-bees brought to California are said to have arrived in San Francisco in March, 1853. A bee-keeper by the name of Shelton purchased a lot, consisting of twelve swarms, from some one at Aspinwall, who had brought them from New York. All the hives contained bees when landed at San Francisco, but they finally dwindled to one hive, which was taken to San José. The little emigrants flourished and multiplied in the bountiful pastures of the Santa Clara valley, sending off three swarms the first sea-

son. The owner was killed shortly afterward, and in settling up his estate, two of the swarms were sold at auction
for one hundred and five and one hundred and ten dollars
respectively. Other importations were made, from time to
time, by way of the Isthmus, and, though great pains were
taken to insure success, about one-half usually died on the
way. Four swarms were brought safely across the plains in
1859, the hives being placed in the rear end of a wagon,
which was stopped in the afternoon to allow the bees to fly
and feed in the floweriest places that were within reach until
dark, when the hives were closed.

In 1855, two years after the time of the first arrivals
from New York, a single swarm was brought over from
San José, and let fly in the Great Central Plain. Bee-culture, however, has never gained much attention there, notwithstanding the extraordinary abundance of honey-bloom
and the high price of honey. A few hives are found here and
there among settlers who chanced to have learned something about the business before coming to the State. But
sheep, cattle, and grain raising are the chief industries, as
they require less skill and care, while the profits thus far
have been greater. In 1856, honey sold here at from one
and a half to two dollars per pound. Twelve years later the
price had fallen to twelve and a half cents. In 1868, I sat
down to dinner with a band of ravenous sheep-shearers at a
ranch on the San Joaquin, where fifteen or twenty hives
were kept, and our host advised us not to spare the large
pan of honey he had placed on the table, as it was the cheap-
est article he had to offer. In all my walks, however, I have

never come upon a regular bee-ranch there like those so common and so skillfully managed in the southern counties of the State. The few pounds of honey and wax produced are consumed at home, and are scarcely taken into account among the coarser products of the farm. The swarms that escape from their careless owners have a weary, perplexing time of it in seeking suitable homes. Most of them make their way to the foot-hills of the mountains, or to the trees that line the banks of the rivers, where some hollow log or trunk may be found. A friend of mine, while out hunting last winter on the San Joaquin, came upon an old coon-trap hidden among some tall grass, near the edge of the river, upon which he sat down to rest. Shortly afterward his attention was forced upon a crowd of angry bees that were flying excitedly about his head, when he discovered that he was sitting upon their hive, which was found to contain more than two hundred pounds of honey. Out in the broad, swampy delta of the Sacramento and San Joaquin the little wanderers have been known to build their combs in a bunch of rushes or stiff, wiry grass, scarcely protected from the weather, and in danger every spring of being carried away by floods. They have the advantage, however, of a vast extent of fresh pasture, accessible only to themselves.

The present condition of the Grand Central Garden is very different from that we have sketched. About ten years ago, when the gold placers had been pretty thoroughly exhausted, the attention of fortune-seekers—not home-seekers—was in great part turned away from the mines to the fertile plains, and many began experiments in a kind of restless, wild-cat agriculture. A load of lumber would be hauled to some spot on the free wilderness where water could be easily found, and a rude box-cabin built. Then a gang-plow was procured, and a dozen mustang ponies, worth ten or fifteen dollars apiece, and with these hundreds of acres were stirred as easily as if the land had been under cultivation for years, tough perennial roots being almost wholly absent. Thus, a ranch was established, and from these bare wooden huts, as centers of desolation, the wild flora vanished in ever-widening circles. But the arch destroyers are the shepherds, with their flocks of hoofed locusts, sweeping over the ground like a fire, and trampling down every rod that escapes the plow as completely as if the whole plain were a cottage garden-plot without a fence. But notwithstanding "a' that," a thousand swarms of bees may be pastured here for every one now gathering honey. The greater portion is still covered every season with a repressed growth of bee-flowers, for most of the species are annuals, and many of them are not relished by sheep or cattle, while the rapidity of their growth enables them to develop and mature their seeds before any foot has time to crush them. The ground is, therefore, kept sweet, and the race is perpetuated, though only as a suggestive shadow of the magnificence of its wildness.

The time will undoubtedly come when the entire area of this noble valley will be tilled like a garden, when the fertilizing waters of the mountains, now flowing to the sea, will be distributed to every acre, giving rise to prosperous towns, wealth, arts, etc. Then, I suppose, there will be few left, even among botanists, to deplore the vanished primeval flora. In the meantime, the pure waste going on—the wanton destruction of the innocents—is a sad sight to see, and the sun may well be pitied in being compelled to look on.

The bee-pastures of the coast ranges last longer and are far more varied than those of the great plain, on account of differences of soil and climate, moisture and shade, etc. Some of the mountains are upward of four thousand feet in height, and small streams and springs, oozy bogs, etc., occur in great abundance and variety in the wooded regions, while open parks flooded with sunshine, and hill-girt valleys lying at different elevations, each with its own peculiar climate and exposure, possess the required conditions for the development of species and families of plants widely varied.

Next [to] the plain there is, first, a series of smooth hills, planted with a rich and showy vegetation that differs but little from that of the plain itself—as if the edge of the plain had been lifted and bent into flowing folds with all its flowers in place, only toned down a little as to their luxuriance, and a few new species introduced, such as the hill lupines, mints, and gilias. The colors show finely when thus held to view on the slopes—patches of red, purple, blue, yellow, and white blending around the edges, the whole appearing at a little distance like a map colored in sections.

Above this lies the park and chaparral region, with evergreen oaks planted wide apart, and blooming shrubs from three to ten feet high—manzanita and ceanothus of several species, mixed with rhamnus, cercis, pickeringia, cherry, amelanchier, and adenostoma, in shaggy, interlocking thickets, with many species of hosackia, clover, monardella, castilleia, etc., in the openings.

The main ranges send out long spurs somewhat parallel to their axes, inclosing level valleys, many of them quite extensive, and containing a great profusion of sun-loving bee-flowers in their wild state; but these are, in great part, already lost to the bees by cultivation.

Nearer the coast are the giant forests of the redwoods, extending from near the Oregon line to Santa Cruz. Beneath the cool, deep shade of these majestic trees the ground is occupied by ferns, chiefly woodwardia and aspidiums, with only a few flowering plants—oxalis, trientalis, erythronium, fritillaria, smilax, and other shade-lovers. But all along the redwood belt there are sunny openings on hill-slopes looking to the south, where the giant trees stand back and give the ground to the small sun-flowers and the bees. Around the lofty redwood walls of these little bee-acres there is usually a fringe of chestnut-oak, laurel, and madroña, the last of which is a surpassingly beautiful tree, and a great favorite with the bees. The trunks of the largest specimens are seven or eight feet thick, and about fifty feet high, the bark crimson and chocolate, the leaves plain, large, and glossy, like those of *Magnolia grandiflora*, while the flowers are white and urn-shaped, in well-proportioned panicles from five to ten inches long. When in full bloom, a single tree seems to be visited at times by a whole hive of bees at once, and the grand hum of such a multitude of wings makes the listener guess that more than the ordinary work of honey-winning must be going on.

How perfectly enchanting and care-obliterating are these withdrawn gardens of the woods—long vistas opening to the sea—sunshine sifting and pouring upon the flowery ground in a tremulous, shifting mosaic, as the light-ways in the leafy wall open and close with the swaying breeze—shining leaves and flowers, birds and bees, mingling together in sprng-time harmony, and nectarous fragrance exhaling from a thousand thousand fountains! In these balmy, dissolving days, when the deep heart-beats of Nature are felt thrilling rocks and trees and everything alike, common business and friends, children and wives, are happily forgotten, and even the natural honey-work of bees, and the care of birds for their young, seems slightly out of place.

To the northward, in Humboldt and the adjacent counties, whole hill-sides are covered with rhododendron, making a glorious melody of bee-bloom in the spring. And the western azalea, hardly less flowery, grows in massy thickets three to eight feet high around the edges of groves and woods as far south as San Luis Obispo, usually accompanied by manzanita, while the valleys, with their varying moisture and shade, yield a rich variety of the smaller honey-flowers, such as mentha, lycopus, micromeria, audibertia, trichostema, and other mints, with vaccinium, wild strawberry, geranium, calais, and golden-rod; and in the cool glens along the stream-banks, where the shade of trees is not too deep, spiræa, dog-wood, photinia, and calycanthus, and many species of rubus, form interlacing tangles, some portion of which continues in bloom for months.

Though the coast region was the first to be invaded and settled by white men, it has suffered less from a bee point of view than either of the other main divisions—chiefly, no doubt, because of the unevenness of the surface, and because it is owned by individuals, instead of lying exposed to the flocks of the "sheepman." These remarks apply more particularly to the north half of the coast. Farther south there is less moisture, less forest shade, and the honey flora is less varied.

The sierra region is the largest of the three main divisions of the bee-lands of the State, and the most regularly varied in its subdivisions, owing to their gradual rise from the level of the Central Plain to the alpine summits. The foot-hill region is about as dry and sunful, from the end of May until the setting in of the winter rains, as the plain. There are no shady forests, no damp glens, at all like those lying at the same elevations in the coast mountains. The social compositæ of the plain, with a few added species, form the bulk of the herbaceous portion of the vegetation up to a height of fifteen hundred feet or more, shaded lightly here and there with oaks and Sabine pines, and interrupted by patches of ceanothus and buckeye. Above this, and just below the forest region, there is a dark, heath-like belt of chaparral, composed almost exclusively of *Adenos-*

toma fasciculata, a bush belonging to the rose family, from five to eight feet high, with small, round leaves in fascicles, and bearing a multitude of small white flowers in panicles on the ends of the upper branches. Where it occurs at all, it usually covers all the ground with a close impenetrable growth, scarcely broken for miles.

Up through the forest region, to a height of about nine thousand feet above sea-level, there are ragged patches of manzanita, and five or six species of ceanothus, called deer-brush or California lilac. These are the most important of all the honey-bearing bushes of the sierra. *Chamæbatia foliolosa*, a little shrub about a foot high, with flowers like the strawberry, makes handsome carpets beneath the yellow pines, and seems to be a favorite with the bees; while the pines themselves furnish unlimited quantities of pollen and honey-dew. The product of a single tree, ripening its pollen at the right time of year, would be sufficient for the wants of a whole hive. Along the streams, there is a rich growth of lilies, larkspurs, pedicularis, castilleias, and clover. The alpine region contains the flowery glacier meadows, and countless small gardens in all sorts of places full of potentilla of several species, spraguea, ivesia, epilobium, and golden-rod, with beds of bryanthus and the charming cassiope covered with sweet bells. Even the tops of the mountains are blessed with flowers,—dwarf phlox, polemonium, ribes, hulsea, etc. I have seen wild bees and butterflies feeding at a height of thirteen thousand feet above the sea. Many, however, that go up these dangerous heights never come down again. Some, undoubtedly, perish in storms, and I have found thousands lying dead or benumbed on the surface of the glaciers, to which they had perhaps been attracted by the white glare. From swarms that escaped their owners in the lowlands, the honey-bee is now generally distributed throughout the whole length of the sierra, up to an elevation of eight thousand feet above sea-level. At this height, where the snow falls to a depth of fifteen or twenty feet, they flourish without care. Even higher than this several bee-trees have been cut which contained over two hundred pounds of honey.

The destructive action of sheep has not been nearly so universal on the mountain pastures as on those of the great plain, but in many places it has been more complete, owing to the more friable character of the soil, and its sloping position. The slant digging and down-raking action of hoofs on the steeper slopes of moraines has uprooted and buried many of the tender plants from year to year, without allowing them time to mature their seeds. The shrubs, too, are badly bitten, especially the various species of ceanothus. Fortunately, neither sheep nor cattle care to feed on the manzanita, spiræa, or adenostoma; and these fine honey-bushes are too stiff and tall, or grow in places too rough and inaccessible, to be trodden under foot. Also the cañon walls and gorges, which form so considerable a part of the area of the range, while inaccessible to domestic sheep, are well fringed with honey-shrubs, and contain thousands of lovely bee-gardens, lying hid in narrow side-cañons and

135

recesses fenced with avalanche taluses, and on the top of flat, projecting headlands where only the bees would think to look for them. But, on the other hand, a great portion of the woody plants that escape the feet and teeth of the sheep are destroyed by the shepherds by means of running fires, which are set everywhere during the dry autumn for the purpose of burning off the old fallen trunks and under-brush, with a view to improving the pastures, and making more open ways for the flocks. These destructive sheep-fires sweep through nearly the entire forest belt of the range, from one extremity to the other, consuming not only the underbrush, but the young trees and seedlings on which the permanence of the forests depends; thus setting in motion a long train of evils which will certainly reach far beyond bees and bee-keepers.

The plow has not yet invaded the forest region to any appreciable extent, neither has it accomplished much in the foot-hills. Thousands of bee-ranches might be established along the margin of the plain, and up to a height of four thousand feet, wherever water could be obtained. The climate at this elevation admits of the making of permanent homes, and by moving the hives to higher pastures as the lower pass out of bloom, the annual yield of honey would be nearly doubled. The foot-hill pastures, as we have seen, fail about the end of May, those of the chaparral belt and lower forests are in full bloom in June, those of the upper and alpine region in July, August, and September. In Scotland, after the best of the Lowland bloom is past, the bees are carried in carts to the Highlands, and set free on the heather hills. In France, too, and in Poland, they are carried from pasture to pasture among orchards and fields in the same way, and along the rivers in barges, to collect the honey of the delightful vegetation of the banks. In Egypt, they are taken far up the Nile, and floated slowly home again, gathering the honey-harvest of the various fields on the way, timing their movements in accord with the seasons. Were similar methods pursued in California, the productive season would extend nearly all the year.

The average elevation of the north half of the sierra is considerably less than that of the south half, and small streams, with the bank and meadow gardens dependent upon them, are less abundant. Around the headwaters of the Yuba, Feather, and Pitt rivers, there are extensive tablelands of lava, sparsely planted with pines, through which the sunshine reaches the ground with little interruption, and here flourishes a scattered, tufted growth of golden applopappus, linosyris, bahia, wyetheia, arnica, artemisia, and similar plants; with manzanita, cherry, plum, and thorn in ragged patches on the cooler hill-slopes. At the extremities of the Great Plain, the sierra and coast ranges curve around and lock together in a labyrinth of mountains and valleys, throughout which the coast and sierra floras are mingled, making at the north, with its temperate climate and copious rain-fall, a perfect paradise for bees— though, strange to say, scarce a single regular bee-ranch has yet been established in it. Cultivation, however, is making rapid headway over all the State, and before long the wild honey-bloom of the mountains will vanish as completely as that of the fertile lowlands.

PART TWO

Regarding Mount Shasta comprehensively from a bee point of view, encircled by its many climates, and sweeping aloft from the torrid plain deep into the cold azure, we find the first five thousand feet from the summit pretty generally snow-clad, and therefore they are about as flowerless and honeyless as the sea. The base of this arctic region is girdled by a belt of naked lava measuring about a thousand feet in vertical breadth. Beautiful lichens enliven the faces of the cliffs with their bright colors, and in some of the warmer nooks of the rocks there are a few tufts of alpine daisies, wall-flowers, and pentstemons; but, notwithstanding these bloom freely in the late summer, the zone as a whole is almost as honeyless as the icy summit, and its lower edge may be taken as the superior limit of the honey-line. Immediately below this comes the forest zone, covered with a rich growth of conifers, chiefly silver firs, rich in pollen and honey-dew, and diversified with countless garden openings, many of them less than a hundred yards across. Next, in orderly succession, comes the grand bee-zone. Its area far surpasses that of the icy summit and both the other zones combined, for it goes sweeping majestically around the entire mountain, with a breadth of six or seven miles and a circumference of nearly a hundred miles.

Shasta, as we have already suggested, is a fire-mountain, created by a succession of eruptions of ashes and molten lava, which, flowing over the lips of its several craters, grew outward and upward like the trunk of a knotty exogenous tree. Then followed a strange contrast. The glacial winter came on, loading the cooling mountain with ice which flowed slowly outward in every direction, radiating from the summit in the form of one vast conical glacier—a down-crawling mantle of ice upon a fountain of smoldering fire, crushing and grinding for centuries its brown, flinty lavas with incessant activity, and thus degrading and remodeling the entire mountain. When, at length, the glacial period began to draw near its close, the ice-mantle was gradually melted off around the bottom, and, in receding and breaking into its present fragmentary condition, irregular rings and heaps of moraine matter were stored upon its flanks. The glacial erosion of most of the Shasta lavas produced a detritus, composed of rough, subangular bowlders of moderate size and porous gravel and sand, which yields freely to the transporting power of running water. Under Nature's management, the next marked geological event made to take place in the history of Mount Shasta was a water-flood of extraordinary magnitude, which acted with sublime energy upon this prepared glacial detritus, sorting it out and carrying down immense quantities from the higher slopes, and redepositing it in smooth, delta-like beds around the base; and it is these

flood-beds of moraine soil, thus suddenly and simultaneously laid down and joined edge to edge, that now form the
main honey-zone.

Thus, by forces seemingly antagonistic and destructive,
has Mother Nature accomplished her beneficent designs—
now a flood of fire, now a flood of ice, now a flood of water;
and then an outburst of organic life, a milky-way of snowy
petals and wings, girdling the rugged mountain like a
cloud, as if the vivifying sunbeams beating against its sides
had broken into a foam of plant-bloom and bees.

In this lovely wilderness the bees rove and revel, rejoicing in the bounty of the sun, clambering eagerly through
bramble and hucklebloom, stirring the clustered bells of
the manzanita, now humming aloft among polleny willows and firs, now down on the ashy ground among gilias
and buttercups, and anon plunging deep into snowy banks
of cherry and buckthorn. They consider the lilies and roll
into them, and, like lilies, they toil not, for they are im-
pelled by sun-power, as water-wheels by water-power; and
when the one has plenty of high-pressure water, the other
plenty of sunshine, they hum and quiver alike. Sauntering
in the bee-lands in the sun-days of summer, one may readily infer the time of day from the comparative energy of
bee-movements alone—drowsy and moderate in the cool
of the morning, increasing in energy with the ascending
sun, and, at high noon, thrilling and quivering in wild
ecstasy, then gradually declining again to the stillness of
night. In my excursions among the glaciers I occasionally
meet bees that are hungry, like mountaineers who venture

too far and remain too long above the bread-line; then they droop and wither like autumn leaves. The Shasta bees are perhaps better fed than any others in the sierra. Their field-work is one perpetual feast; but, however exhilarating the sunshine or bountiful the supply of flowers, they are always dainty feeders. Humming-moths and humming-birds seldom set foot upon a flower, but poise on the wing in front of it, and reach forward as if they were sucking through straws. But bees, though as dainty as they, hug their favorite flowers with profound cordiality, and push their blunt, polleny faces against them, like babies on their mother's bosom. And fondly, too, with eternal love, does Mother Nature clasp her small bee-babies, and suckle them, multitudes at once, on her warm Shasta breast.

Besides the common honey-bee there are many other species here—fine mossy, burly fellows, who were nourished on the mountains thousands of sunny seasons before the advent of the domestic species. Among these are the bumble-bees, mason-bees, carpenter-bees, and leaf-cutters. Butterflies, too, and moths of every size and pattern,—some broad-winged like bats, flapping slowly, and sailing in easy curves; others like small, flying violets, shaking about loosely in short, crooked flights close to the flowers, feasting luxuriously night and day. Great numbers of deer also delight to dwell in the brushy portions of the bee-pastures.

Bears, too, roam the sweet wildness, their blunt, shaggy forms harmonizing well with the trees and tangled bushes, and with the bees, also, notwithstanding the disparity in

size. They are fond of all good things, and enjoy them to
the utmost, with but little troublesome discrimination—
flowers and leaves as well as berries, and the bees themselves as well as their honey. Though the California bears
have as yet had but little experience with honey-bees, they
often succeed in reaching their bountiful stores, and it
seems doubtful whether bees themselves enjoy honey with
so great a relish. By means of their powerful teeth and
claws they can gnaw and tear open almost any hive conveniently accessible. Most honey-bees, however, in search of
a home are wise enough to make choice of a hollow in a
living tree, a considerable distance above the ground,
when it is possible; then they are pretty secure, for though
the smaller black and brown bears climb well, they are
unable to break into strong hives while compelled to exert
themselves to keep from falling, and at the same time to
endure the stings of the fighting bees without having their
paws free to rub them off. But woe to the black bumble-
bees discovered in their mossy mouse-nests in the ground!
The bears with a few strokes of their huge paws lay the
entire establishment bare, and, before time is given for a
general buzz, bees old and young, larvæ, honey, stings,
nest, and all are taken in in one ravishing mouthful.

Not the least influential of the agents concerned in the
superior sweetness of the Shasta flora are its storms—
storms I mean that are strictly local, bred and born on the
mountain, and belonging to it as completely as its vegetation. The magical rapidity with which they grow on the
mountaintop, and bestow their charity in rain and snow,

never fails to astonish the inexperienced low-lander. Often in calm, glowing days, while the bees are still on the wing, a storm-cloud may be seen far above in the pure ether, swelling its pearl bosses, and growing silently like a plant. Presently a clear, ringing discharge of thunder is heard, then a rush of wind, sounding over the bending woods like the roar of the ocean, and mingling rain, snow-flowers, honey-flowers, and bees in wild storm harmony.

Still more impressive are the warm, reviving days of spring in the mountain pastures. The blood of the plants throbbing beneath the life-giving sunshine seems to be heard and felt. Plant growth goes on before our eyes, and every tree in the woods, and bush, and flower is seen as a hive of restless industry. The deeps of the sky are mottled with singing wings of every tone and color; clouds of brilliant chrysididæ dancing and swirling in exquisite rhythm, golden-barred vespidæ, dragon-flies, butterflies, grating cicadas, and jolly, rattling grasshoppers, fairly enameling the light.

On bright, crisp mornings a striking optical effect may frequently be observed from the shadows of the higher mountains while the sunbeams are pouring past overhead. Then every insect, no matter what may be its own proper color, burns white in the light. Gauzy-winged hymenoptera, moths, jet-black beetles, all are transfigured alike in pure, spiritual white, like snowflakes.

In southern California, where bee-culture has had so much skillful attention of late years, the pasturage is not more abundant, or more advantageously varied as to the

number of its honey plants and their distribution over
mountain and plain, than that of many other portions of
the State where the industrial currents flow in other channels. The famous white sage (*Audibertia*), belonging to the
mint family, flourishes here in all its glory, blooming in
May, and yielding great quantities of clear, pale honey,
which is greatly prized in every market it has yet reached.
This species grows chiefly in the valleys and low hills. The
black sage on the mountains is part of a dense, thorny chaparral, which is composed chiefly of adenostoma, ceanothus, manzanita, and cherry—not differing greatly from
that of the southern portion of the sierra, but more dense
and continuous, and taller, and remaining longer in
bloom. Stream-side gardens, so charming a feature of both
the sierra and coast mountains, are less numerous but exceedingly rich in honey flowers wherever found: melilotus,
columbine, collinsia, verbena, zauschneria, wild rose,
honeysuckle, philadelphus, and lilies rising from the
warm, moist dells in a very storm of exuberance. Wild
buckwheat of many species is developed in great abundance over the dry, sandy valleys and lower slopes of the
mountains toward the end of summer, and is at this time
the main dependence of the bees, reënforced here and there
by orange groves, alfalfa fields, and small home gardens.

The main honey months in ordinary seasons are April,
May, June, July, and August; while the other months are
usually flowery enough to yield sufficient for the bees.

According to Mr. J. T. Gordon, president of the Los
Angeles County Bee-keepers' Association, the first bees in-

troduced into the county were a single hive, which cost $150 in San Francisco and arrived in September, 1854.* In April of the following year this hive sent out two swarms, which were sold for one hundred dollars each. From this small beginning the bees gradually multiplied to about three thousand swarms in the year 1873. In 1876, it was estimated that there were between fifteen and twenty thousand hives in the county, producing an annual yield of about one hundred pounds to the hive—in some exceptional cases a much greater yield.

In San Diego County, at the beginning of the season of 1878, there were about 24,000 hives, and the shipments from the one port of San Diego for the same year, from July 17th to November 10th, were 1,071 barrels, 15,544 cases, and nearly ninety tons. The largest bee-ranches have about a thousand hives, and are carefully and skillfully managed, every scientific appliance of merit being brought into use. There are few bee-keepers, however, who own half as many as this, or who give their undivided attention to the business. Orange culture at present heavily overshadows every other business.

A good many of the so-called bee-ranches of Los Angeles and San Diego counties are still of the rudest pioneer kind imaginable. A man unsuccessful in everything else hears the interesting story of the profits and comforts of

---

*Fifteen hives of Italian bees were introduced into Los Angeles County in 1855, and in 1876 they had increased to five hundred. The marked superiority claimed for them over the common species is now attracting considerable attention.

bee-keeping, and concludes to try it, buys a few colonies, or gets them from some overstocked ranch on shares, takes them back to the foot of some cañon where the pasturage is fresh, squats on the land, with or without the permission of the owner, sets up his hives, makes a box cabin for himself scarcely bigger than a bee-hive, and awaits his fortune.

Bees suffer sadly from famine during the dry years which occasionally occur in the southern and middle portions of the State. If the rain-fall amounts only to three or four inches, instead of from twelve to twenty as in ordinary seasons, then sheep and cattle die in thousands, and so do these small winged cattle, unless they are carefully fed, or removed to other pastures. The year 1877 will long be remembered as exceptionally rainless and distressing. Scarce a flower bloomed on the dry valleys away from the stream-sides, and not a single grain-field depending upon rain was reaped. The seed only sprouted, and came up a little way, and withered; and horses, cattle, and sheep grew thinner day by day, nibbling at bushes and weeds along the shallowing edges of streams, many of which were dried up altogether for the first time since the settlement of the country.

In the course of a trip made during the summer of that year through Monterey, San Luis Obispo, Santa Barbara, Ventura, and Los Angeles counties, the deplorable effects of the drought were everywhere visible—leafless fields, dead and dying cattle, dead bees, and half-dead people with dusty, doleful faces. Even the birds and squirrels were in distress, though their suffering was less painfully

apparent than that of the poor cattle. These were falling
one by one in slow, sure starvation along the banks of the
hot, sluggish streams, while thousands of buzzards corre-
spondingly fat were sailing above them, or standing
gorged on the ground beneath the trees, waiting with easy
faith for fresh carcasses. The quails, prudently considering
the hard times, abandoned all thought of pairing off. They
were too poor to marry, and so continued in flocks all
through the year without attempting to rear young. In riding three hundred miles not a single brood of young was
seen, though the breeding season was past; but, on the contrary, all the old ones were still in flocks. The ground-
squirrels, though an exceptionally industrious and enterprising race, as every farmer knows, were hard pushed for
a living; not a fresh leaf or seed was to be found save in the
trees, whose bossy masses of dark green foliage presented a
striking contrast to the ashen baldness of the ground beneath them. The squirrels, leaving their accustomed feeding-grounds, betook themselves to the leafy oaks to gnaw
out the acorn stores of the provident woodpeckers, but the
latter kept up a vigilant watch upon their movements. I
noticed four woodpeckers in league against one squirrel,
driving the poor fellow out of an oak that they claimed. He
dodged round the knotty trunk from side to side, as nimbly
as he could in his famished condition, only to find a sharp
bill everywhere. But the fate of the bees that year seemed
the saddest of them all. From one-half to three-fourths of
them died, in different portions of Los Angeles and San
Diego counties, of sheer starvation—not less than eighteen

thousand colonies in these two counties alone, while in the adjacent counties the death-rate was hardly less.

Even the colonies nearest to the mountains suffered more or less this year, for the smaller vegetation on the foot-hills was affected by the drought almost as severely as that of the valleys and plains, and even the hardy, deep-rooted chaparral, the surest dependence of the bees, bloomed sparingly, while much of it was beyond reach. All could have been saved, however, by promptly supplying them with food when their own stores began to fail, and before they became enfeebled and discouraged, or by cutting roads back into the mountains, and taking them into the heart of the flowery chaparral. The Santa Lucia, San Rafael, San Gabriel, San Jacinto, and San Bernardino ranges are almost untouched as yet save by the wild bees. Some idea of their resources, and of the advantages and disadvantages they offer to bee-keepers, may be formed from an excursion that I made into the San Gabriel range about the beginning of August of "the dry year." This range, containing most of the characteristic features of the other ranges just mentioned, overlooks the Los Angeles vineyards and orange groves from the north, and is more rigidly inaccessible in the ordinary meaning of the word than any other that I ever attempted to penetrate. The slopes are exceptionally steep and insecure to the foot, and they are covered with thorny bushes from five to ten feet high. With the exception of little spots not visible in general views, the entire surface is covered with them, massed in close hedge growth, sweeping gracefully down into

The Bee-Pastures of California

every gorge and hollow, and swelling over every ridge and summit in shaggy, ungovernable exuberance, offering more honey to the acre for half the year than the most crowded clover-field in bloom time. But when beheld from the open San Gabriel valley, beaten with dry sunshine, all that was seen of the range seemed to wear a forbidding aspect. From base to summit all seemed gray, barren, silent, its glorious chaparral appearing like dry moss creeping over its dull, wrinkled ridges and hollows.

Setting out from Pasadena, a hopeful little colony of orange groves about six miles from the city of Los Angeles, I reached the foot of the range about sundown; and being weary and heated with my walk across the shadeless plain, concluded to camp for the night. After resting a few moments I began to look about among the flood-bowlders of the creek for a smooth camp-ground, when I came upon a strange, dark-looking man who had been chopping cordwood. He seemed greatly surprised at seeing me, so I sat down with him on the live-oak log he had been cutting, and made haste to give a reason for my appearance in his solitude, explaining that I was anxious to find out something about the mountains and meant to make my way up Eaton Creek next morning. Then he kindly invited me to camp with him, and led me to his little cabin, situated at the foot of the first of the mountain slopes, where a small spring oozes out of a bank overgrown with wild rose-bushes. After supper, when the daylight was gone, he explained that he was out of candles, so we sat in the dark, while he gave me a sketch of his life in a mixture of Spanish and

149

* Insects *

English. He was born in Mexico, his father Irish, his mother Spanish. He had been a miner, rancher, prospecter, hunter, etc., rambling always, and wearing his life away in mere waste, but now he was going to settle down. His past life, he said, was of "no account," but the future was promising. He was going to "make money and marry a Spanish woman." People mine here for water as for gold. He had been running a tunnel into a spur of the mountain back of his cabin. "My prospect is good," he said, "and if I chance to strike a good strong flow, I'll soon be worth five or ten thousand dollars. For that flat out there," referring to a small, irregular patch of bowldery detritus, two or three acres in size, that had been deposited by Eaton Creek during some flood season,—"that flat is large enough for a nice orange grove, and the bank behind the cabin will do for a vineyard, and after watering my own trees and vines I will have some left to sell to my neighbors below me down the valley. And then," he continued, "I can keep bees and make money that way, too, for the mountains above here are just full of honey in the summer time, and one of my neighbors down here says that he will let me have a whole lot of hives on shares to start with. You see I've a good thing; I'm all right now." All this prospective affluence in the sunken, bowlder-choked flood-bed of a mountain stream! Leaving the bees out of the count, most fortune-seekers would as soon think of settling on the summit of Mount Shasta.

About half an hour's walk above the cabin is "The Fall," famous throughout the valley settlements as the finest yet discovered in the range. It is a charming little thing, with a low, sweet voice, singing like a bird as it pours from a notch in a short ledge some thirty-five or forty feet into a round-mirror pool. The face of the cliff back of it and on both sides is smoothly covered and embossed with mosses, against which the white water shines out in showy relief, like a silver instrument in a velvet case. Hither come the San Gabriel lads and lasses to gather ferns and dabble away their hot holidays in the cool water, glad to escape from their commonplace palm gardens and orange groves. The delicate maiden-hair grows on fissured rocks within reach of the spray, while broad-leaved maples and sycamores cast soft, mellow shade over a rich profusion of bee-flowers growing among bowlders in front of the pool—the fall, the flowers, the bees, the ferny rocks and leafy shade forming a charming little poem of wildness, the last of a series extending down the flowery slopes of San Antonio through the rugged, foam-beaten bosses of the main Eaton cañon.

From the base of the fall I followed the ridge that forms the western rim of the Eaton basin to the summit of one of the principal peaks, which is about five thousand feet above sea level. Then, turning eastward, I crossed the middle of the basin, forcing a way over its many subordinate ridges and across its eastern rim, having to contend almost everywhere with the floweriest and most impenetrable growth of honey bushes I had ever encountered since first my mountaineering began. Most of the Shasta chaparral is leafy nearly to the ground; here the main stems are naked for three or four feet, and interspiked with dead twigs, forming a stiff *chevaux de frise* through which even the bears make their way with difficulty. I was compelled to creep for miles on all-fours, and in following the bear-trails often found tufts of hair on the bushes where they had forced themselves through.

For a hundred feet or so above the fall the ascent was made possible only by tough cushions of club-moss that clung to the rock. Above this the ridge weathers away to a thin knife-blade for a few hundred yards, and thence to the summit of the range it carries a bristly mane of chaparral. Here and there small openings occur on rocky places, commanding fine views across the cultivated valley to the ocean. These I found by the tracks were favorite outlooks and resting-places for the wild animals—bears, wolves, foxes, wild-cats, etc.—which abound here, and would have to be taken into account in the establishment of bee-ranches. In the deepest thickets I found wood-rat villages—groups of huts four to six feet high, built of sticks and leaves in rough, tapering piles, like musk-rat cabins. I noticed a good many bees, too, most of them wild. The tame honey-bees seemed languid and wing-weary, as if they had come all the way up from the flowerless plain.

After reaching the summit I had time to make only a hasty survey of the basin, now glowing in the sunset gold, before hastening down into one of the tributary cañons in search of water. Emerging from a particularly tedious breadth of chaparral, I found myself free and erect in a beautiful park-like grove of live-oak, the ground planted with aspidiums and brier-roses, while the glossy foliage made a close canopy overhead, leaving the gray dividing trunks bare to show the beauty of their plain, interlacing arches. The bottom of the cañon was dry where I first reached it, but a bunch of scarlet mimulus indicated water at no great distance, and I soon discovered about a bucketful in the hollow of the rock. This, however, was full of dead bees, wasps, beetles, and leaves, well steeped and simmered in the hot sunshine, and would, therefore, require boiling and filtering through fresh charcoal before it could be made available. Tracing the dry channel about a mile farther down to its junction with a larger tributary cañon, I at length discovered a lot of bowlder pools, clear as crystal, brimming full, and linked together by glistening streamlets just strong enough to sing audibly. Flowers in full bloom adorned their margins, lilies ten feet high, larkspurs, columbines, and luxuriant ferns, leaning and overarching in lavish abundance, while a noble old live-oak spread its rugged arms over all. Here I camped, making my bed on smooth cobble-stones.

Next day, in the channel of a tributary that heads on Mount San Antonio, I passed about fifteen or twenty gardens like the one in which I slept—lilies in every one of them, in the full pomp of bloom. My third camp was made near the middle of the general basin, at the head of a long system of cascades from ten to two hundred feet high, one following the other in close succession down a rocky, inaccessible cañon, making a total descent of nearly seventeen hundred feet. Above the cascades the stream passes through a series of open, sunny levels, the largest of which are about an acre in size, where the wild bees and their companions were feasting on a fine, showy growth of zauschneria, painted cups, and monardella; and gray squirrels were busy harvesting the burs of the Douglass spruce, the only conifer I met in the basin.

The eastern slopes of the basin are in every way similar to those we have described, and the same may be said of other portions of the range. From the highest summit, far as the eye could reach, the landscape was one vast bee-pasture, a rolling wilderness of honey bloom, scarcely broken by bits of forest or the rocky outcrops of hill-tops and ridges.

Beyond the San Bernardino range lies the wild "sagebrush country," bounded on the east by the Colorado River, and extending in a general northerly direction to Nevada and along the eastern base of the Sierra beyond Mono Lake.

The greater portion of this immense region, including Owens Valley, Death Valley, and the Sink of the Mohave, and whose area is nearly one-fifth that of the entire State, is usually regarded as a desert, not because of any lack in the soil, but for want of rain, and rivers available for irrigation. Very little of it, however, is desert in the eyes of a bee.

Looking now over all the available pastures of the State, it appears that the business of bee-keeping is still in its infancy. Even in the more enterprising of the southern counties, where so vigorous a beginning has been made, less than a tenth of their honey resources have as yet been developed; while in the Great Plain, the coast ranges, the

Sierra Nevada, and the northern region about Mount Shasta, the business can hardly be said to exist at all. What the limits of its developments in the future may be, with the advantages of cheaper transportation and the invention of better methods in general, it is not easy to guess. Nor, on the other hand, are we able to measure the influence on bee interests likely to follow the destruction of the forests, now rapidly falling before fire and the ax. As to the sheep evil, that can hardly become greater than it is at the present day. In short, notwithstanding the wide-spread deterioration and destruction of every kind already effected, California, with her incomparable climate and flora, is still the best of all the bee-lands of the world.

CHAPTER FIVE

✷

PREDATORS

Nowhere is John Muir's foresightedness more evident than in his essays on carnivores. In his day, even those who were concerned with protecting animals dismissed predators as aberrant villains. But Muir was writing about the rights of bears as early as 1872, anticipating the biocentrism of Aldo Leopold by sixty years. His reflections on the rabbit hunt demonstrate a remarkable understanding of the necessity of meat-eaters. Muir's refusal to judge predators by human standards is best exemplified in his essay on the shrike, whose attack on the young gophers was presented without reproach. Similarly, he did not condemn the snake's taste for frogs, for this reptile would in turn become prey, thus maintaining the "balance of Nature."

The following essays reveal more than Muir's concern for the health of ecosystems. He believed that snakes, hawks, and coyotes exist for their own sakes as well. Our anthropocentrism, he points out in the final selection of this book, prevents us from recognizing this fact. To the modern reader, Muir's insistence that animals are individuals in their own right is perhaps the most striking feature of his writings.

Bears

THE SIERRA BEAR, BROWN OR GRAY, THE sequoia of the animals, tramps over all the Park,* though few travelers have the pleasure of seeing him. On he fares through the majestic forests and cañons, facing all sorts of weather, rejoicing in his strength, everywhere at home, harmonizing with the trees and rocks and shaggy chaparral. Happy fellow! his lines have fallen in pleasant places,—lily gardens in silver-fir forests, miles of bushes in endless variety and exuberance of bloom over hill-waves and valleys and along the banks of streams, cañons full of music and waterfalls, parks fair as Eden,—places in which one might expect to meet angels rather than bears.

In this happy land no famine comes nigh him. All the year round his bread is sure, for some of the thousand kinds

*Yosemite.

that he likes are always in season and accessible, ranged on
the shelves of the mountains like stores in a pantry. From
one to another, from climate to climate, up and down he
climbs, feasting on each in turn,—enjoying as great variety as if he traveled to far-off countries north and south. To
him almost every thing is food except granite. Every tree
helps to feed him, every bush and herb, with fruits and
flowers, leaves and bark; and all the animals he can catch—
badgers, gophers, ground squirrels, lizards, snakes, etc.,
and ants, bees, wasps, old and young, together with their
eggs and larvae and nests. Craunched and hashed, down all
go to his marvelous stomach, and vanish as if cast into a
fire. What digestion! A sheep or a wounded deer or a pig
he eats warm, about as quickly as a boy eats a buttered
muffin; or should the meat be a month old, it still is welcomed with tremendous relish. After so gross a meal as
this, perhaps the next will be strawberries and clover, or
raspberries with mushrooms and nuts, or puckery acorns
and chokecherries. And as if fearing that anything eatable
in all his dominions should escape being eaten, he breaks
into cabins to look after sugar, dried apples, bacon, etc.
Occasionally he eats the mountaineer's bed; but when he
has had a full meal of more tempting dainties he usually
leaves it undisturbed, though he has been known to drag it
up through a hole in the roof, carry it to the foot of a tree,
and lie down on it to enjoy a siesta. Eating everything,
never is he himself eaten except by man, and only man is
an enemy to be feared. "B'ar meat," said a hunter from

whom I was seeking information, "b'ar meat is the best meat in the mountains; their skins make the best beds, and their grease the best butter. Biscuit shortened with b'ar grease goes as far as beans; a man will walk all day on a couple of them biscuit."

In my first interview with a Sierra bear we were frightened and embarrassed, both of us, but the bear's behavior was better than mine. When I discovered him, he was standing in a narrow strip of meadow, and I was concealed behind a tree on the side of it. After studying his appearance as he stood at rest, I rushed toward him to frighten him, that I might study his gait in running. But, contrary to all I had heard about the shyness of bears, he did not run at all; and when I stopped short within a few steps of him, as he held his ground in a fighting attitude, my mistake was monstrously plain. I was then put on my good behavior, and never afterward forgot the right manners of the wilderness.

This happened on my first Sierra excursion in the forest to the north of Yosemite Valley. I was eager to meet the animals, and many of them came to me as if willing to show themselves and make my acquaintance; but the bears kept out of my way.

An old mountaineer, in reply to my questions, told me that bears were very shy, all save grim old grizzlies, and that I might travel the mountains for years without seeing one, unless I gave my mind to them and practiced the stealthy ways of hunters. Nevertheless, it was only a few weeks after I had received this information that I met the one mentioned above, and obtained instruction at first-hand.

I was encamped in the woods about a mile back of the rim of Yosemite, beside a stream that falls into the valley by way of Indian Cañon. Nearly every day for weeks I went to the top of the North Dome to sketch; for it commands a general view of the valley, and I was anxious to draw every tree and rock and waterfall. Carlo, a St. Bernard dog, was my companion,—a fine, intelligent fellow that belonged to a hunter who was compelled to remain all summer on the hot plains, and who loaned him to me for the season for the sake of having him in the mountains, where he would be so much better off. Carlo knew bears through long experience, and he it was who led me to my first interview, though he seemed as much surprised as the bear at my unhunter-like behavior. One morning in June, just as the sunbeams began to stream through the trees, I set out for a day's sketching on the dome; and before we had gone half a mile from camp Carlo snuffed the air and looked cautiously ahead, lowered his bushy tail, drooped his ears, and began to step softly like a cat, turning every few yards and looking me in the face with a telling expression, saying plainly enough, "There is a bear a little way ahead." I walked carefully in the indicated direction, until I approached a small flowery meadow that I was familiar with, then crawled to the foot of a tree on its margin, bearing in mind what I had been told about the shyness of bears. Looking out cautiously over the instep of the tree, I saw a big, burly cinnamon bear about thirty yards off, half erect, his paws resting on the trunk of a fir that had fallen into the meadow, his hips almost buried in grass and flowers. He was listening attentively and trying to catch the scent, showing that in some way he was aware of our approach. I watched his gestures, and tried to make the most of my opportunity to learn what I could about him, fearing he would not stay long. He made a fine picture, standing alert in the sunny garden walled in by the most beautiful firs in the world.

After examining him at leisure, noting the sharp muzzle thrust inquiringly forward, the long shaggy hair on his broad chest, the stiff ears nearly buried in hair, and the slow, heavy way in which he moved his head, I foolishly made a rush on him, throwing up my arms and shouting to frighten him, to see him run. He did not mind the demonstration much; only pushed his head farther forward, and looked at me sharply as if asking, "What now? If you want to fight, I'm ready." Then I began to fear that on me would fall the work of running. But I was afraid to run, lest he should be encouraged to pursue me; therefore I held my ground, staring him in the face within a dozen yards or so, putting on as bold a look as I could, and hoping the influence of the human eye would be as great as it is said to be. Under these strained relations the interview seemed to last a long time. Finally, the bear, seeing how still I was, calmly withdrew his huge paws from the log, gave me a piercing look, as if warning me not to follow him, turned, and walked slowly up the middle of the meadow into the

* Predators *

forest; stopping every few steps and looking back to make sure that I was not trying to take him at a disadvantage in a rear attack. I was glad to part with him, and greatly enjoyed the vanishing view as he waded through the lilies and columbines.

Thenceforth I always tried to give bears respectful notice of my approach, and they usually kept well out of my way. Though they often came around my camp in the night, only once afterward, as far as I know, was I very near one of them in daylight. This time it was a grizzly I met; and as luck would have it, I was even nearer to him than I had been to the big cinnamon. Though not a large specimen, he seemed formidable enough at a distance of less than a dozen yards. His shaggy coat was well grizzled, his head almost white. When I first caught sight of him he was eating acorns under a Kellogg oak, at a distance of perhaps seventy-five yards, and I tried to slip past without disturbing him. But he had either heard my steps on the gravel or caught my scent, for he came straight toward me, stopping every rod or so to look and listen: and as I was afraid to be seen running, I crawled on my hands and knees a little way to one side and hid behind a libocedrus, hoping he would pass me unnoticed. He soon came up opposite me, and stood looking ahead, while I looked at him, peering past the bulging trunk of the tree. At last, turning his head, he caught sight of mine, stared sharply a minute or two, and then, with fine dignity, disappeared in a manzanita-covered earthquake talus.

Considering how heavy and broad-footed bears are, it is

wonderful how little harm they do in the wilderness. Even in the well-watered gardens of the middle region, where the flowers grow tallest, and where during warm weather the bears wallow and roll, no evidence of destruction is visible. On the contrary, under nature's direction, the massive beasts act as gardeners. On the forest floor, carpeted with needles and brush, and on the tough sod of glacier meadows, bears make no mark; but around the sandy margin of lakes their magnificent tracks form grand lines of embroidery. Their well-worn trails extend along the main cañons on either side, and though dusty in some places make no scar on the landscape. They bite and break off the branches of some of the pines and oaks to get the nuts, but this pruning is so light that few mountaineers ever notice it; and though they interfere with the orderly lichen-veiled decay of fallen trees, tearing them to pieces to reach the colonies of ants that inhabit them, the scattered ruins are quickly pressed back into harmony by snow and rain and over-leaning vegetation.

The number of bears that make the Park their home may be guessed by the number that have been killed by the two best hunters, Duncan and old David Brown. Duncan began to be known as a bear-killer about the year 1865. He was then roaming the woods, hunting and prospecting on the south fork of the Merced. A friend told me that he killed his first bear near his cabin at Wawona; that after mustering courage to fire he fled, without waiting to learn the effect of his shot. Going back in a few hours he found poor Bruin dead, and gained courage to try again. Duncan

* Predators *

confessed to me, when we made an excursion together in
1875, that he was at first mortally afraid of bears, but after
killing a half dozen he began to keep count of his victims,
and became ambitious to be known as a great bear-hunter.
In nine years he had killed forty-nine, keeping count by
notches cut on one of the timbers of his cabin on the shore
of Crescent Lake, near the south boundary of the Park. He
said the more he knew about bears, the more he respected
them and the less he feared them. But at the same time he
grew more and more cautious, and never fired until he had
every advantage, no matter how long he had to wait and
how far he had to go before he got the bear just right as to
the direction of the wind, the distance, and the way of escape in case of accident; making allowance also for the
character of the animal, old or young, cinnamon or grizzly. For old grizzlies, he said, he had no use whatever, and
he was mighty careful to avoid their acquaintance. He
wanted to kill an even hundred; then he was going to con-
fine himself to safer game. There was not much money in
bears, anyhow, and a round hundred was enough for glory.

I have not seen or heard of him lately, and do not know
how his bloody count stands. On my excursions, I occasionally passed his cabin. It was full of meat and skins hung
in bundles from the rafters, and the ground about it was
strewn with bones and hair,—infinitely less tidy than a
bear's den. He went as hunter and guide with a geological
survey party for a year or two, and was very proud of the
scientific knowledge he picked up. His admiring fellow
mountaineers, he said, gave him credit for knowing not

only the botanical names of all the trees and bushes, but also the "botanical names of the bears."

The most famous hunter of the region was David Brown, an old pioneer, who early in the gold period established his main camp in a little forest glade on the north fork of the Merced, which is still called "Brown's Flat." No finer solitude for a hunter and prospector could be found; the climate is delightful all the year, and the scenery of both earth and sky is a perpetual feast. Though he was not much of a "scenery fellow," his friends say that he knew a pretty place when he saw it as well as any one, and liked mightily to get on the top of a commanding ridge to "look off."

When out of provisions, he would take down his old-fashioned long-barreled rifle from its deer-horn rest over the fireplace and set out in search of game. Seldom did he have to go far for venison, because the deer liked the wooded slopes of Pilot Peak ridge, with its open spots where they could rest and look about them, and enjoy the breeze from the sea in warm weather, free from troublesome flies, while they found hiding-places and fine aromatic food in the deer-brush chaparral. A small, wise dog was his only companion, and well the little mountaineer understood the object of every hunt, whether deer or bears, or only grouse hidden in the fir-tops. In deer-hunting Sandy had little to do, trotting behind his master as he walked noiselessly through the fragrant woods, careful not to step heavily on dry twigs, scanning open spots in the chaparral where the deer feed in the early morning and toward sunset, peering

over ridges and swells as new outlooks were reached, and
along alder and willow fringed flats and streams, until he
found a young buck, killed it, tied its legs together, threw
it on his shoulder, and so back to camp. But when bears
were hunted, Sandy played an important part as leader, and
several times saved his master's life; and it was as a bear-
hunter that David Brown became famous. His method, as
I had it from a friend who had passed many an evening in
his cabin listening to his long stories of adventure, was
simply to take a few pounds of flour and his rifle, and go
slowly and silently over hill and valley in the loneliest part
of the wilderness, until little Sandy came upon the fresh
track of a bear, then follow it to the death, paying no heed
to time. Wherever the bear went he went, however rough
the ground, led by Sandy, who looked back from time to
time to see how his master was coming on, and regulated
his pace accordingly, never growing weary or allowing any
other track to divert him. When high ground was reached
a halt was made, to scan the openings in every direction,
and perchance Bruin would be discovered sitting upright
on his haunches, eating manzanita berries; pulling down
the fruit-laden branches with his paws and pressing them
together, so as to get substantial mouthfuls, however mixed
with leaves and twigs. The time of year enabled the hunter
to determine approximately where the game would be
found: in spring and early summer, in lush grass and clover
meadows and in berry tangles along the banks of streams,
or on pea-vine and lupine clad slopes; in late summer and
autumn, beneath the pines, eating the cones cut off by the

squirrels, and in oak groves at the bottom of cañons, munching acorns, manzanita berries, and cherries; and after snow had fallen, in alluvial bottoms, feeding on ants and yellow-jacket wasps. These food places were always cautiously approached, so as to avoid the chance of sudden encounters.

"Whenever," said the hunter, "I saw a bear before he saw me, I had no trouble in killing him. I just took lots of time to learn what he was up to and how long he would be likely to stay, and to study the direction of the wind and the lay of the land. Then I worked round to leeward of him, no matter how far I had to go; crawled and dodged to within a hundred yards, near the foot of a tree that I could climb, but which was too small for a bear to climb. There I looked well to the priming of my rifle, took off my boots so as to climb quickly if necessary, and, with my rifle in rest and Sandy behind me, waited until my bear stood right, when I made a sure, or at least a good shot back of the fore leg. In case he showed fight, I got up the tree I had in mind, before he could reach me. But bears are slow and awkward with their eyes, and being to windward they could not scent me, and often I got in a second shot before they saw the smoke. Usually, however, they tried to get away when they were hurt, and I let them go a good safe while before I ventured into the brush after them. Then Sandy was pretty sure to find them dead; if not, he barked bold as a lion to draw attention, or rushed in and nipped them behind, enabling me to get to a safe distance and watch a chance for a finishing shot.

* Predators *

"Oh yes, bear-hunting is a mighty interesting business, and safe enough if followed just right, though, like every other business, especially the wild kind, it has its accidents, and Sandy and I have had close calls at times. Bears are nobody's fools, and they know enough to let men alone as a general thing, unless they are wounded, or cornered, or have cubs. In my opinion, a hungry old mother would catch and eat a man, if she could; which is only fair play, anyhow, for we eat them. But nobody, as far as I know, has been eaten up in these rich mountains. Why they never tackle a fellow when he is lying asleep I never could understand. They could gobble us mighty handy, but I suppose it's nature to respect a sleeping man."

Sheep-owners and their shepherds have killed a great many bears, mostly by poison and traps of various sorts. Bears are fond of mutton, and levy heavy toll on every flock driven into the mountains. They usually come to the corral at night, climb in, kill a sheep with a stroke of the paw, carry it off a little distance, eat about half of it, and return the next night for the other half; and so on all summer, or until they are themselves killed. It is not, however, by direct killing, but by suffocation through crowding against the corral wall in fright, that the greatest losses are incurred. From ten to fifteen sheep are found dead, smothered in the corral, after every attack; or the walls are broken, and the flock is scattered far and wide. A flock may escape the attention of these marauders for a week or two in the spring; but after their first taste of the fine mountain-fed meat the visits are persistently kept up, in spite of all precautions. Once I spent a night with two Portuguese shepherds, who were greatly troubled with bears, from two to four or five visiting them almost every night. Their camp was near the middle of the Park, and the wicked bears, they said, were getting worse and worse. Not waiting now until dark, they came out of the brush in broad daylight, and boldly carried off as many sheep as they liked. One evening, before sundown, a bear, followed by two cubs, came for an early supper, as the flock was being slowly driven toward the camp. Joe, the elder of the shepherds, warned by many exciting experiences, promptly climbed a tall tamarack pine, and left the freebooters to help themselves; while Antone, calling him a coward, and declaring that he was not going to let bears eat up his sheep before his face, set the dogs on them, and rushed toward them with a great noise and a stick. The frightened cubs ran up a tree, and the mother ran to meet the shepherd and dogs. Antone stood astonished for a moment, eying the oncoming bear; then fled faster than Joe had, closely pursued. He scrambled to the roof of their little cabin, the only refuge quickly available; and fortunately, the bear, anxious about her young, did not climb after him,—only held him in mortal terror a few minutes, glaring and threatening, then hastened back to her cubs, called them down, went to the frightened, huddled flock, killed a sheep, and feasted in peace. Antone piteously entreated cautious Joe to show him a good safe tree, up which he climbed like a sailor climbing a mast, and held on as long as he could with legs crossed, the slim pine recommended by Joe being nearly branchless. "So you, too, are a bear coward as well as Joe," I said, after hearing the story. "Oh, I tell you," he replied, with grand solemnity, "bear face close by look awful; she just as soon eat me as not. She do so as eef all my sheeps b'long every one to her own self. I run to bear no more. I take tree every time."

After this the shepherds corraled the flock about an hour before sundown, chopped large quantities of dry wood and made a circle of fires around the corral every night, and one with a gun kept watch on a stage built in a pine by the side of the cabin, while the other slept. But after the first night or two this fire fence did no good, for the robbers seemed to regard the light as an advantage, after becoming used to it.

On the night I spent at their camp the show made by the wall of fire when it was blazing in its prime was magnificent,—the illumined trees round about relieved against solid darkness, and the two thousand sheep lying down in one gray mass, sprinkled with gloriously brilliant gems, the effect of the firelight in their eyes. It was nearly midnight when a pair of the freebooters arrived. They walked boldly through a gap in the fire circle, killed two sheep, carried them out, and vanished in the dark woods, leaving ten dead in a pile, trampled down and smothered against the corral fence; while the scared watcher in the tree did not fire a single shot, saying he was afraid he would hit some of the sheep, as the bears got among them before he could get a good sight.

In the morning I asked the shepherds why they did not

move the flock to a new pasture. "Oh, no use!" cried Antone. "Look my dead sheeps. We move three four time
before, all the same bear come by the track. No use. To-
morrow we go home below. Look my dead sheeps. Soon
all dead."

Thus were they driven out of the mountains more than a
month before the usual time. After Uncle Sam's soldiers,
bears are the most effective forest police, but some of the
shepherds are very successful in killing them. Altogether,
by hunters, mountaineers, Indians, and sheepmen, probably five or six hundred have been killed within the bounds
of the Park, during the last thirty years. But they are not in
danger of extinction. Now that the Park is guarded by soldiers, not only has the vegetation in great part come back
to the desolate ground, but all the wild animals are increasing in numbers. No guns are allowed in the Park except
under certain restrictions, and after a permit has been obtained from the officer in charge. This has stopped the bar-
barous slaughter of bears, and especially of deer, by
shepherds, hunters, and hunting tourists, who, it would
seem, can find no pleasure without blood.

The Coyote

THE CALIFORNIA WOLF OR COYOTE IS
a beautiful animal, graceful in motion, dark gray or yellowish in color, with erect ears, a sharp muzzle, and a
handsome bushy tail reaching to the ground. In size he is
about equal to the English shepherd dog. His bark is rather musical, sharp and whistly but not at all admired by
shepherds. With the exception of man he is by far the most
destructive of California mutton-eating animals, and of
course is cordially disliked by mutton owners.

With rare caution and boldness he spies out the exposed
edges of a flock, estimating from some hilltop the relative
positions of sheep, shepherd, and dog, biding his time
though pressed by hunger, crouching in the chaparral
of the mountain or tarweeds of the plain, until his ripe

opportunity arrives, when by night or day he takes his chosen lamb in so masterly a manner that oftentimes neither sheep nor shepherd are aware of his presence among them.

Lizards and Rattlesnakes

A GREAT VARIETY OF LIZARDS ENLIVEN the warm portions of the Park.* Some of them are more than a foot in length, others but little larger than grass-hoppers. A few are snaky and repulsive at first sight, but most of the species are handsome and attractive, and bear acquaintance well; we like them better the farther we see into their charming lives. Small fellow mortals, gentle and guileless, they are easily tamed, and have beautiful eyes, expressing the clearest innocence, so that, in spite of prej-udices brought from cool, lizardless countries, one must soon learn to like them. Even the horned toad of the plains and foothills, called horrid, is mild and gentle, with charm-ing eyes, and so are the snakelike species found in the un-derbrush of the lower forests. These glide in curves with

*Yosemite.

all the ease and grace of snakes, while their small, undeveloped limbs drag for the most part as useless appendages. One specimen that I measured was fourteen inches long, and as far as I saw it made no use whatever of its diminutive limbs.

Most of them glint and dart on the sunny rocks and across open spaces from bush to bush, swift as dragonflies and humming-birds, and about as brilliantly colored. They never make a long-sustained run, whatever their object, but dart direct as arrows for a distance of ten or twenty feet, then suddenly stop, and as suddenly start again. These stops are necessary as rests, for they are short-winded, and when pursued steadily are soon run out of breath, pant pitifully, and may easily be caught where no retreat in bush or rock is quickly available.

If you stay with them a week or two and behave well, these gentle saurians, descendants of an ancient race of giants, will soon know and trust you, come to your feet, play, and watch your every motion with cunning curiosity. You will surely learn to like them, not only the bright ones, gorgeous as the rainbow, but the little ones, gray as lichened granite, and scarcely bigger than grasshoppers; and they will teach you that scales may cover as fine a nature as hair or feathers or anything tailored.

There are many snakes in the cañons and lower forests, but they are mostly handsome and harmless. Of all the tourists and travelers who have visited Yosemite and the adjacent mountains, not one has been bitten by a snake of any sort, while thousands have been charmed by them.

* Predators *

Some of them vie with the lizards in beauty of color and dress patterns. Only the rattlesnake is venomous, and he carefully keeps his venom to himself as far as man is concerned, unless his life is threatened.

Before I learned to respect rattlesnakes I killed two, the first on the San Joaquin plain. He was coiled comfortably around a tuft of bunch-grass, and I discovered him when he was between my feet as I was stepping over him. He held his head down and did not attempt to strike, although in danger of being trampled. At that time, thirty years ago, I imagined that rattlesnakes should be killed wherever found. I had no weapon of any sort, and on the smooth plain there was not a stick or a stone within miles; so I crushed him by jumping on him, as the deer are said to do. Looking me in the face he saw I meant mischief, and quickly cast himself into a coil, ready to strike in defense. I knew he could not strike when traveling, therefore I threw handfuls of dirt and grass sods at him, to tease him out of coil. He held his ground a few minutes, threatening and striking, and then started off to get rid of me. I ran forward and jumped on him; but he drew back his head so quickly my heel missed, and he also missed his stroke at me. Persecuted, tormented, again and again he tried to get away, bravely striking out to protect himself; but at last my heel came squarely down, sorely wounding him, and a few more brutal stampings crushed him. I felt degraded by the killing business, farther from heaven, and I made up my mind to try to be at least as fair and charitable as the snakes themselves, and to kill no more save in self-defense.

* Lizards and Rattlesnakes *

The second killing might also, I think, have been avoided, and I have always felt somewhat sore and guilty about it. I had built a little cabin in Yosemite, and for convenience in getting water, and for the sake of music and society, I led a small stream from Yosemite Creek into it. Running along the side of the wall it was not in the way, and it had just fall enough to ripple and sing in low, sweet tones, making delightful company, especially at night when I was lying awake. Then a few frogs came in and made merry with the stream,—and one snake, I suppose to catch the frogs.

Returning from my long walks, I usually brought home a large handful of plants, partly for study, partly for ornament, and set them in a corner of the cabin, with their stems in the stream to keep them fresh. One day, when I picked up a handful that had begun to fade, I uncovered a large coiled rattler that had been hiding behind the flowers. Thus suddenly brought to light face to face with the rightful owner of the place, the poor reptile was desperately embarrassed, evidently realizing that he had no right in the cabin. It was not only fear that he showed, but a good deal of downright bashfulness and embarrassment, like that of a more than half honest person caught under suspicious circumstances behind a door. Instead of striking or threatening to strike, though coiled and ready, he slowly drew his head down as far as he could, with awkward, confused kinks in his neck and a shamefaced expression, as if wishing the ground would open and hide him. I have looked into the eyes of so many wild animals that I feel sure I did not mistake the feelings of this unfortunate snake. I did not want to kill him, but I had many visitors, some of them children, and I oftentimes came in late at night; so I judged he must die.

Since then I have seen perhaps a hundred or more in these mountains, but I have never intentionally disturbed them, nor have they disturbed me to any great extent, even by accident, though in danger of being stepped on. Once, while I was on my knees kindling a fire, one glided under the arch made by my arm. He was only going away from the ground I had selected for a camp, and there was not the slightest danger, because I kept still and allowed him to go in peace. The only time I felt myself in serious danger was when I was coming out of the Tuolumne Cañon by a steep side cañon toward the head of Yosemite Creek. On an earthquake talus, a boulder in my way presented a front so high that I could just reach the upper edge of it while standing on the next below it. Drawing myself up, as soon as my head was above the flat top of it I caught sight of a coiled rattler. My hands had alarmed him, and he was ready for me; but even with this provocation, and when my head came in sight within a foot of him, he did not strike. The last time I sauntered through the big cañon I saw about two a day. One was not coiled, but neatly folded in a narrow space between two cobblestones on the side of the river, his head below the level of them, ready to shoot up like a Jack-in-the-box for frogs or birds. My foot spanned the space above within an inch or two of his head, but he only held it lower. In making my way through a particularly tedious tangle of buckthorn, I parted the branches on the side of an open spot and threw my bundle of bread into it; and when, with my arms free, I was pushing through after it, I saw a small rattlesnake dragging his tail from beneath my bundle. When he caught sight of me he eyed me angrily, and with an air of righteous indignation seemed to be asking why I had thrown that stuff on him. He was so small that I was inclined to slight him, but he struck out so angrily that I drew back, and approached the opening from the other side. But he had been listening, and when I looked through the brush I found him confronting me, still with a come-in-if-you-dare expression. In vain I tried to explain that I only wanted my bread; he stoutly held the ground in front of it; so I went back a dozen rods and kept still for half an hour, and when I returned he had gone.

One evening, near sundown, in a very rough, boulder-choked portion of the cañon, I searched long for a level spot for a bed, and at last was glad to find a patch of flood-sand on the riverbank, and a lot of driftwood close by for a campfire. But when I threw down my bundle, I found two snakes in possession of the ground. I might have passed the night even in this snake den without danger, for I never knew a single instance of their coming into camp in the night; but fearing that, in so small a space, some late comers, not aware of my presence, might get stepped on when I was replenishing the fire, to avoid possible crowding I encamped on one of the earthquake boulders.

The Shrike

BEFORE THE ARRIVAL OF FARMERS IN the Wisconsin woods the small ground squirrels, called "gophers," lived chiefly on the seeds of wild grasses and weeds, but after the country was cleared and ploughed no feasting animal fell to more heartily on the farmer's wheat and corn. Increasing rapidly in numbers and knowledge, they became very destructive, especially in the spring when the corn was planted, for they learned to trace the rows and dig up and eat the three or four seeds in each hill about as fast as the poor farmers could cover them. And unless great pains were taken to diminish the numbers of the cunning little robbers, the fields had to be planted two or three times over, and even then large gaps in the rows would be found. The loss of the grain they consumed after it was ripe, together with the winter stores laid up in their burrows, amounted to little as compared with the loss of the seed on which the whole crop depended.

One evening about sundown, when my father sent me out with the shotgun to hunt them in a stubble field, I learned something curious and interesting in connection with these mischievious gophers, though just then they were doing no harm. As I strolled through the stubble watching for a chance for a shot, a shrike flew past me and alighted on an open spot at the mouth of a burrow about thirty yards ahead of me. Curious to see what he was up to, I stood still to watch him. He looked down the gopher hole in a listening attitude, then looked back at me to see if I was coming, looked down again and listened, and looked back at me. I stood perfectly still, and he kept twitching his tail, seeming uneasy and doubtful about venturing to do the savage job that I soon learned he had in his mind. Finally, encouraged by my keeping so still, to my astonishment he suddenly vanished in the gopher hole.

A bird going down a deep narrow hole in the ground like a ferret or a weasel seemed very strange, and I thought it would be a fine thing to run forward, clap my hand over the hole, and have the fun of imprisoning him and seeing what he would do when he tried to get out. So I ran forward but stopped when I got within a dozen or fifteen yards of the hole, thinking it might perhaps be more interesting to wait and see what would naturally happen without my interference. While I stood there looking and listening, I heard a great disturbance going on in the burrow, a mixed lot of keen squeaking, shrieking, distressful cries, telling

that down in the dark something terrible was being done.
Then suddenly out popped a half-grown gopher, four and
a half or five inches long, and, without stopping a single
moment to choose a way of escape, ran screaming through
the stubble straight away from its home, quickly followed
by another and another, until some half-dozen were driven
out, all of them crying and running in different directions
as if at this dreadful time home, sweet home, was the most
dangerous and least desirable of any place in the wide
world. Then out came the shrike, flew above the runaway
gopher children, and, diving on them, killed them one
after another with blows at the back of the skull. He then
seized one of them, dragged it to the top of a small clod so
as to be able to get a start, and laboriously made out to fly
with it about ten or fifteen yards, when he alighted to rest.
Then he dragged it to the top of another clod and flew with
it about the same distance, repeating this hard work over
and over again until he managed to get one of the gophers
on to the top of a log fence. How much he ate of his hard-
won prey, or what he did with the others, I can't tell, for by
this time the sun was down and I had to hurry home to my
chores.

The Jackrabbit Hunt

THE JACKRABBIT OF THE LOWLANDS, especially on the open foothills of the great San Joaquin and Sacramento valleys, were comparatively rare when California was wild, but as soon as flocks and herds of cattle multiplied and cornfields and orchards furnished food for rabbits, the numbers of these rodents increased. At the same time the animals that preyed upon rabbits, in particular the coyote and golden eagle and large gopher snakes, were destroyed, the coyotes because they occasionally killed a lamb or a calf, or an old sheep when it became feeble.

A reward of as much as ten dollars a scalp and for a long time five dollars was put on the coyote to insure their destruction. Every sheep-owner and cattle-owner spread strychnine beside. As for the golden eagle, who used to live on jackrabbits chiefly, he was shot simply because he was a bird of prey, although he did no harm to the farmer, while the snake because he was a snake was also killed. Of course, as soon as the balance of Nature was disturbed there was a rapid increase of rabbits, one species over another. Because of the destruction of the enemies of the California hares and the increase in the amount of food, their numbers multiplied until they threatened to consume every blade of grass, wheat or oats, and all the fruit of the orchards and vineyards as well. Then in desperate self-defense the farmers combined to shoot and poison and destroy, but all without avail. They continued to increase more than ever until at last they found it necessary to build high corrals or pens with walls much higher than the hares could jump, and with wings half a mile to a mile long, spreading wider and wider. Then all the neighbors, old and young, male and female, boys and girls, assembled, some on horseback, some in their carriages, many afoot, all under the command of leaders, who spread them out and encircled large spaces, gradually driving the hares together, then started them down the long lane which became gradually narrower and narrower and terminated in the corral. Oftentimes many thousands were thus captured at a single drive.

A similar difficulty was encountered in the coast range valleys where first one might hunt for weeks without seeing a single Douglas or spermophile. By killing off the snakes and hawks and coyotes which fed upon them, they multiplied so rapidly, food being furnished them in greater and greater abundance as the farms and fields increased and as the orchards came into bearing and supplied them with

The Jackrabbit Hunt

delicious fruit, that they threatened to consume everything, just as had occurred in the great central valley, requiring tens of thousands of dollars every year in a vain attempt to exterminate them with strychnine, or with smoke or poisonous gases, but all without avail. The loss of a few chickens from hawks and a few calves and sheep from coyotes amounted to nothing compared with the toll levied on everything that was produced by the spermophiles— the penalty for interfering with the balance of Nature in this manner.

Anthropocentrism
and Predation

THE WORLD, WE ARE TOLD, WAS MADE
especially for man—a presumption not supported by all
the facts. A numerous class of men are painfully astonished
whenever they find anything, living or dead, in all God's
universe, which they cannot eat or render in some way what
they call useful to themselves. They have precise dogmatic
insight of the intentions of the Creator, and it is hardly
possible to be guilty of irreverence in speaking of *their* God
any more than of heathen idols. He is regarded as a civilized, law-abiding gentleman in favor either of a republi-
can form of government or of a limited monarchy; believes
in the literature and language of England; is a warm sup-
porter of the English constitution and Sunday schools and
missionary societies; and is as purely a manufactured article as any puppet of a half-penny theater.

* Anthropocentrism and Predation *

With such views of the Creator it is, of course, not surprising that erroneous views should be entertained of the creation. To such properly trimmed people, the sheep, for example, is an easy problem—food and clothing "for us," eating grass and daisies white by divine appointment for this predestined purpose, on perceiving the demand for wool that would be occasioned by eating of the apple in the Garden of Eden.

In the same pleasant plan, whales are storehouses of oil for us, to help out the stars in lighting our dark ways until the discovery of the Pennsylvania oil wells. Among plants, hemp, to say nothing of the cereals, is a case of evident destination for ships' rigging, wrapping packages, and hanging the wicked. Cotton is another plain case of clothing. Iron was made for hammers and ploughs, and lead for bullets; all intended for us. And so of other small handfuls of insignificant things.

But if we should ask these profound expositors of God's intentions, How about those man-eating animals—lions, tigers, alligators—which smack their lips over raw man? Or about those myriads of noxious insects that destroy labor and drink his blood? Doubtless man was intended for food and drink for all these? Oh, no! Not at all! These are unresolvable difficulties connected with Eden's apple and the Devil. Why does water drown its lord? Why do so many minerals poison him? Why are so many plants and fishes deadly enemies? Why is the lord of creation subjected to the same laws of life as his subjects? Oh, all these things are satanic, or in some way connected with the first garden.

✳ Predators ✳

Now, it never seems to occur to these far-seeing teachers that Nature's object in making animals and plants might possibly be first of all the happiness of each one of them, not the creation of all for the happiness of one. Why should man value himself as more than a small part of the one great unit of creation? And what creature of all that the Lord has taken the pains to make is not essential to the completeness of that unit—the cosmos? The universe would be incomplete without man; but it would also be incomplete without the smallest transmicroscopic creature that dwells beyond our conceitful eyes and knowledge.

From the dust of the earth, from the common elementary fund, the Creator has made *Homo sapiens*. From the same material He has made every other creature, however noxious and insignificant to us. They are earth-born companions and our fellow mortals. The fearfully good, the orthodox, of this laborious patchwork of modern civilization cry "Heresy" on every one whose sympathies reach a single hair's breadth beyond the boundary epidermis of our own species. Not content with taking all of earth, they also claim the celestial country as the only ones who possess the kind of souls for which that imponderable empire was planned.

This star, our own good earth, made many a successful journey around the heavens ere man was made, and whole kingdoms of creatures enjoyed existence and returned to dust ere man appeared to claim them. After human beings have also played their part in Creation's plan, they too may disappear without any general burning or extraordinary commotion whatever.

Plants are credited with but dim and uncertain sensation, and minerals with positively none at all. But why may not even a mineral arrangement of matter be endowed with sensation of a kind that we in our blind exclusive perfection can have no manner of communication with?

But I have wandered from my object. I stated a page or two back that man claimed the earth was made for him, and I was going to say that venomous beasts, thorny plants, and deadly diseases of certain parts of the earth prove that the whole world was not made for him. When an animal from a tropical climate is taken to high latitudes, it may perish of cold, and we say that such an animal was never intended for so severe a climate. But when man betakes himself to sickly parts of the tropics and perishes, he cannot see that he was never intended for such deadly climates. No, he will rather accuse the first mother of the cause of the difficulty, though she may never have seen a fever district; or will consider it a providential chastisement for some self-invented form of sin.

Furthermore, all uneatable and uncivilizable animals, and all plants which carry prickles, are deplorable evils which, according to closet researches of clergy, require the cleansing chemistry of universal planetary combustion. But more than aught else mankind requires burning, as being in great part wicked, and if that transmundane furnace can be so applied and regulated as to smelt and purify

Predators

us into conformity with the rest of the terrestrial creation, then the tophetization of the erratic genus *Homo* were a consummation devoutly to be prayed for. But, glad to leave these ecclesiastical fires and blunders, I joyfully return to the immortal truth and immortal beauty of Nature.

Sources

"The Wild Sheep of California," from *Overland Monthly* 12 (April 1874): 358–63.

"Deer," from *Our National Parks* (Boston: Houghton Mifflin, 1901; reprint ed., Madison: University of Wisconsin Press, 1981), pp. 188–93.

"Rodents," from *Our National Parks* (Boston: Houghton Mifflin, 1901; reprint ed., Madison: University of Wisconsin Press, 1981), pp. 194–204.

Unpublished manuscript, John Muir Papers, Holt-Atherton Center for Western Studies, University of the Pacific, Stockton, Calif.

"Animal Death," from *The Story of My Boyhood and Youth* (Boston: Houghton Mifflin, 1913; reprint ed., Madison: University of Wisconsin Press, 1965), pp. 106–10.

"Among the Birds of the Yosemite," from *Our National Parks* (Boston: Houghton Mifflin, 1901; reprint ed., Madison: University of Wisconsin Press, 1981), pp. 213–40.

"The Passenger Pigeon," from *The Story of My Boyhood and Youth* (Boston: Houghton Mifflin, 1913; reprint ed., Madison: University of Wisconsin Press, 1965), pp. 128–34.

"Stickeen: An Adventure with a Dog and a Glacier," from *Travels in Alaska* (Boston: Houghton Mifflin, 1915), pp. 246–57. See also longer version in *Stickeen* (Boston: Houghton Mifflin, 1909).

* Sources *

"Cats and Dogs," from *The Story of My Boyhood and Youth* (Boston: Houghton Mifflin, 1913; reprint ed., Madison: University of Wisconsin Press, 1965), pp. 63–69.

"Horses," from *The Story of My Boyhood and Youth* (Boston: Houghton Mifflin, 1913; reprint ed., Madison: University of Wisconsin Press, 1965), pp. 84–89.

"The Grasshopper," from *My First Summer in the Sierra* (Boston: Houghton Mifflin, 1916), pp. 139–41.

"Ants," from *My First Summer in the Sierra* (Boston: Houghton Mifflin, 1916), pp. 43–47.

"The Bee-Pastures of California," from *Century Magazine*, June 1882, pp. 222–29, and July 1882, pp. 388–96.

"Bears," from *Our National Parks* (Boston: Houghton Mifflin, 1901; reprint ed., Madison: University of Wisconsin Press, 1981), pp. 172–88.

Unpublished manuscript, John Muir Papers, Holt-Atherton Center for Western Studies, University of the Pacific, Stockton, Calif.

"Lizards and Rattlesnakes," from *Our National Parks* (Boston: Houghton Mifflin, 1901; reprint ed., Madison: University of Wisconsin Press, 1981), pp. 204–10.

"The Shrike," from *The Story of My Boyhood and Youth* (Boston: Houghton Mifflin, 1913; reprint ed., Madison: University of Wisconsin Press, 1965), pp. 156–58.

Unpublished manuscript, John Muir Papers, Holt-Atherton Center for Western Studies, University of the Pacific, Stockton, Calif.

"Anthropocentrism and Predation," from *A Thousand-Mile Walk to the Gulf* (Boston: Houghton Mifflin, 1916), pp. 136–41.

Illustrations from *Picturesque California*, edited by John Muir (San Francisco: J. Dewing Company, 1887).